has gained insight about prayer on his knees, not behind a lectern. The frequent stories reveal David's journey in this school of prayer. The book is a jackhammer of exhortations, and it pounded away at my stony heart, hitting it from one side, then another, breaking it up until I surrendered to the call to deepen my commitment to intercession as a lifestyle. Golden quotes gleaned from others who have traveled this road of intercession and fasting are woven through the fabric of his own insights.

How many seminars or conferences have you and I attended in which people talked much about prayer, but did little praying? This book is rare in that it invites the reader after each discourse to pray scripted prayers in response to the truth. The author is unwilling to risk that the reader will prayerfully engage the content when the last page is concluded. At first, I viewed these prayers as speed bumps, interrupting my reading, but then the truth broke in on my heart. David was not going to let this be an intellectual exercise. As truth convicted my heart, I found the prayers necessary to process my journey through the pages. I have dabbled in fasting, and often with the wrong motives. This book has changed my view of fasting and challenged me to practice fasting for the right reasons and in regular seasons.

Larry Lane
Director Revival Road Ministries
Senior Fellow Project Pray
530-520-6997
www.revivalroad.net

UNLEASHING THE SUPER NATURAL

THE EXTRAORDINARY POWER OF PRAYER AND FASTING

DAVID F. NIXON

Copyright ©2025 by David F. Nixon

©2025 Dust Jacket Press
Unleashing the Supernatural: The Extraordinary Power of Prayer and Fasting

ISBN: 978-1-953285-51-5

All rights reserved. No part of this publication may be reproduced, distributed, or transmitted in any form or by any means, including photocopying, recording, or other electronic or mechanical methods, without the prior written permission of the publisher, except in the case of brief quotations embodied in critical reviews and certain other noncommercial uses permitted by copyright law. For permission requests, write to the publisher, addressed at the address below:

Dust Jacket Press
P.O. Box 721243
Oklahoma City, OK 73172

Ordering information for print editions:
Quantity sales. Special discounts are available on quantity purchases by corporations, associations, and others. For details, check out at www.dustjacket.com

Individual sales. Dust Jacket Press publications are available through most bookstores. They can also be ordered directly from Dust Jacket: Tel: (800) 495-0192; Email: info@dustjacket.com; www.dustjacket.com

Dust Jacket logos are registered trademarks of Dust Jacket Press, Inc.

All Scripture quotations, unless otherwise indicated, are taken from the Holy Bible, New International Version®, NIV®. Copyright ©1973, 1978, 1984, 2011 by Biblica, Inc.™ Used by permission of Zondervan. All rights reserved worldwide. www.zondervan.com. The "NIV" and "New International Version" are trademarks registered in the United States Patent and Trademark Office by Biblica, Inc.™

Scripture quotations marked "KJV" are taken from the King James Version of the Holy Bible.

Cover design: D.E. West - www.emoondesigns.com
Interior design: Stephanie Booth-Varnado - www.emoondesigns.com

Printed in the United States of America

www.dustjacket.com

ENDORSEMENTS

I wholeheartedly endorse the book, *Unleashing the Supernatural* by my good friend, Dr. David Nixon. Having served alongside Dr. Nixon in ministry for many years, I can testify to his deep wisdom, unwavering faith, and powerful spiritual insights. This book on prayer and fasting is not just a theological exploration, but a practical, soul-stirring guide to drawing closer to God through these vital spiritual disciplines. The author shares insights and lessons from a lifetime of ministry and experience in how God moves in answer to our prayers. The design of the book can serve as a daily devotional guide and daily prayers or as a challenging study of prayer and fasting.

Unleashing the Supernatural offers a clear pathway to cultivate a deeper, more intimate relationship with God. Through both biblical teaching and personal anecdotes, Dr. Nixon invites us into the transformative power of prayer and fasting—not as isolated practices, but as essential rhythms that shape our spiritual lives and align our hearts with God's will.

Whether you are new Christian or have been walking in the faith for many years, this book will challenge, encourage, and equip you to pursue these practices with renewed passion and purpose. I highly recommend it to anyone seeking to grow in their faith and experience the powerful presence of God in a new and profound way. I personally will be using the book to deepen my commitment to unleashing the power of God in my personal life, my family, and my ministry for the glory of God and the building of God's Kingdom.

Dr. David Graves
General Superintendent Emeritus
Church of the Nazarene

Dr. David Nixon stands as a remarkable yet often unsung hero in the realms of prayer and faith. His career spans across various roles including being a successful pastor, a denominational executive, an author, a conference speaker, and a dedicated family man. Throughout these roles, he has maintained a humble and approachable demeanor.

His latest book is a compelling read, with chapters interspersed with prayer responses that urge readers to engage deeply. Dr. Nixon generously cites prayer and church leaders, enriching the book with authoritative insights. The text challenges readers at various points, calling into question our tendencies towards prayerlessness and reliance on self-sufficiency typical in American culture.

Filled with inspirational stories, the book is designed for flexible reading—suitable for consuming in comprehensive sittings or in incremental segments. It encourages readers to delve deeper, eagerly advancing to the next section, principle, or story. The book meets a spectrum of needs: it challenges us to engage in prayer, inspires belief in the importance of prayer, motivates personal growth, and invites us to join God in His mission.

P. Douglas Small
President Project Pray

I have read many books on prayer, but few on fasting. I am not sure if that reflects the lack of writing on the subject or my avoidance of the topic. I confess my skepticism as I approached reading this work, not that I questioned David's sincerity or ambition to take on such a subject, but another book on prayer?

The first chapters on prayer are great. The second section on fasting is gold. The final chapters expand to address relevant needs in the Church as viewed by a seasoned pastor and Church leader. It is clear, wise, practical, and inspiring. It is written by a pastor, not a theologian. He is not a theoretician but a practitioner. And since prayer is not a practice that can be learned in a sermon, I want to listen to one who

DEDICATION

This book is dedicated to Generation Z. Your enthusiasm and vision inspire hope for a world that you are sure to help shape. As you move forward, I encourage you to embrace the age-old spiritual practices that have been handed down through generations. These traditions provide a foundation of faith and wisdom that can guide you as you pursue your dreams and establish yourselves as transformative leaders. Remember, the spiritual disciplines that have enriched the lives of many before you can also empower you to become impactful change-makers for a brighter tomorrow.

CONTENTS

Foreword xi

Overview xv

1. Refuse to Fly Solo 1
2. Unleashing the Supernatural 25
3. How to Operate at Full Capacity 49
4. From Lip Service to Life Change 69
5. Accessing the Miraculous 91
6. Unlocking the Power of God 113
7. Fasting Rocks Your World! 135
8. Expanding Your Faith Horizon 157
9. Miraculous Breakthroughs 179

Afterword 195

FOREWORD

From Genesis to Revelation, the Bible is a testament to the power of ordinary people praying extraordinary prayers. From the dawn of time, God's people have "called on the name of the Lord" (Genesis 4:26). Even before the birth of Israel, His people were marked by their devotion to prayer. Imagine the humble group of believers in the Upper Room, waiting, praying, and then being overwhelmingly filled with the promised Holy Spirit (Acts 1). May we once again rise to the call of prayer, yearning for a moment in history replete with stories of mighty prayer movements spearheaded by humble, devoted hearts, leaving a legacy for generations to come.

From the first book to the last, the Bible stands as a testament to the transformative power of ordinary people engaging in extraordinary prayers. Since the beginning, followers of God have "called on the name of the Lord" (Genesis 4:26). Even before Israel was established, the faithful demonstrated a profound commitment to prayer. Consider the humble believers in the Upper Room who, filled with anticipation, prayed fervently and received the Holy Spirit as promised (Acts 1). Let us be inspired to recommit to fervent prayer and fasting, striving to be part of a historical moment enriched with powerful prayer movements led by hearts humble yet devoted, creating a legacy for future generations.

With deep sorrow and urgency, I must express a concerning observation: prayer is often acknowledged in theory yet tragically neglected in practice. Despite Jesus' heartfelt call for His Church to be a house of prayer (Matthew 21), and the early church's relentless dedication to prayerful gatherings (Acts 1:14), many American congregations now lack genuine, heartfelt prayer, and hardly ever fasting. David poignantly warns, "Prayerless leaders produce prayerless followers." Churches have transformed into venues of preaching and singing, sidelining the foundational power of prayer. The Church is in dire need of a seismic revival, reawakening to the immense privilege and duty of prayer. David's message is a piercing call, urging each reader to deepen their personal prayer life and to inspire communal engagement in this sacred practice.

Reflecting on Israel's forty-year journey through the wilderness, Moses highlighted their legacy of prayer: *"For what great nation has a god as near to them as the Lord our God whenever we call on him?"* (Deuteronomy 4:7, NLT). This underscores the profound nature of prayer—God is irresistibly drawn to the pleas of His people. When we pray, we invite God's presence, often described as the "glory of God," to manifest among us. P.F. Bresee, founder of the Church of the Nazarene, frequently spoke of this divine presence as the "Shekinah Glory." Tragically, churches devoid of prayer rarely experience encounters with the Risen Christ, reducing the concept of holiness to mere doctrine rather than a divine encounter. David reminds us of Bresee's vision: that every church become a house of prayer and a center of divine fire, preserving and empowering the practice of Scriptural holiness.

The undeniable power of extraordinary prayer and fasting has profoundly shaped my life and ministry. Unified prayer invites God's nearness. Early in my ministry, a prayer meeting at the Brooklyn Tabernacle profoundly moved me. Motivated by this, I led my struggling congregation through an intensive prayer initiative characterized by deep repentance. After six months, our church was revitalized by the Lord's overwhelming presence, resulting in miraculous transformations as drug addicts, prostitutes, strippers, and gang members found salvation, deliverance, and freedom. Such miracles are to be expected in response to fervent prayer and fasting.

Indeed, when we restore the altar of prayer, God responds with heavenly fire. When Elijah repaired the neglected altar, his prayers summoned God's consuming fire, sparking a revival marked by genuine repentance and commitment (1 Kings 18). Our churches today desperately need this fresh heavenly fire. But first, we must restore the altar of prayer. David's invitation in this book, with the prophetic zeal of Elijah, challenges us to restore prayer in our homes and churches.

David's anointed writings reveal the potent promises of prayer. Through prayer, miracles unfold, mountains move, and revival erupts. David asserts, "Extraordinary prayer yields extraordinary results." Churches infused with prayer can experience the transformative power evident in the Book of Acts. Prayers from individuals and congregations release God's power, advancing the Gospel globally. The early believers' prayers prevailed against formidable challenges. God remains unchanged. As David eloquently notes, miracles, signs, and wonders are the assured outcomes of devoted prayer. To witness a Revival and Awakening that shakes the foundations, dispels darkness, and heralds an extraordinary end-time harvest, we must commit anew to prayer and fasting.

Let us seize this crucial moment with passionate fervor.

Corey Jones, Lead Pastor
Crossroads Tabernacle

OVERVIEW

Do you feel like your prayers are ordinary? Maybe, you feel like your prayers don't go further than the ceiling. As we delve into the stories of ordinary individuals whose lives were touched by the miraculous, we see a pattern emerge—a testament to the potency of sincere prayer and dedication through fasting. These are not tales of saints or people bestowed with special divine favor but narratives of everyday individuals who chose to reach out through prayer and fasting to address the seemingly impossible.

Such stories serve as vital reminders that the spiritual disciplines of prayer and fasting are accessible and effective for everyone. They are not just spiritual exercises but are invitations to set the stage for God to work miraculously in our lives. By sharing these experiences, I hope you feel inspired to approach your prayer life with a renewed vigor and a belief that the impossible can manifest. Through your earnest prayers and fasting, you too can partake in the unfolding of God's extraordinary works.

The power of prayer is undeniable. Amazing things happen when we pray that happen in no other way. This should ramp up individual or personal praying and draw us into the joy and delight of praying together with others. Imagine the incredible impact that the united, ongoing prayers of many righteous individuals, each dedicated to fasting and seeking divine intervention, could have. Miracles happen. Mountains are moved. Revival comes. The course of nations is changed. Extraordinary prayer leads to remarkable outcomes. This book will reveal that if you truly want to transform your life, incorporating fasting into your spiritual practices can make a significant difference. Ezra and Nehemiah from the Old Testament are powerful examples of how extraordinary prayer can lead to remarkable change.

Ezra received approval from King Cyrus to lead exiles back to Jerusalem, with the king even offering troops for protection. However, feeling ashamed to ask for soldiers, Ezra declined the offer. Instead, he called for a fast, urging everyone to humble themselves before God (8:21). Believing that God's protection is for those who worship Him, Ezra chose not to rely on human assistance. He encouraged the people to pray and fast for their journey. So, what was the outcome of their extraordinary prayers?

> *"So we fasted and earnestly prayed that our God would take care of us, And He heard our prayer." (Ezra 8:23)*

Nehemiah exemplifies extraordinary prayer in a high-pressure situation (Neh. 4:4-11). In just nine verses, he fervently prays, touching God's heart through humility, brokenness, and fasting. Nehemiah's prayer reminds us of the need for quick action in some of our frustrations. Desperate times require supernatural intervention. When Nehemiah, a Persian official, learns of his people's dire condition, he immediately turns to prayer. For him, prayer is a first response, not a last resort. He demonstrates humility and brokenness, sitting down, weeping, mourning, and fasting. Ultimately, the posture of his heart matters more than his voice or physical position. God emphasizes the heart, even as we are created as unified beings—body, soul, and spirit. "All of our various components feed and affect all the others," according to the Kendrick's in *The Battle Plan of Prayer*. They are exactly right to remind us that "posture isn't everything … neither "mandatory nor specifically prescribed."[1]

Whatever position you assume as you read and meditate, whether sitting or standing or kneeling, humbly bow your heart. Kendrick's again: "Whatever posture we employ, may it be "a clear expression of (our) worship, love, devotion, and submission," never just going through the motions of religion. Yes, Lord, "turn even my posture of prayer into a means of steadying my wandering mind and opening my ears to Your voice."[2]

---

1 Stephen and Alex Kendrick, The Battle Plan of Prayer (Nashville: B&H, 2016) 62.
2 Ibid., Kendrick, 66.

The key to touching the heart of God in prayer seems to be the attitude and spirit of prayer. Things like arrogance, pretense, manipulation, bitterness, lack of forgiveness, or a lack of faith, hinder our prayers. Our own attitudes and actions may lock us out. But if we seek the Lord in humility and repentance, with fervency and repentance, with faith and expectation, there is assurance that we can be as close to God as possible, and we can receive what we ask and need. So, perhaps our beginning prayer should be, "Lord, open me up so You can work without hindrance in and through me. I'm ready to hear about the great and mighty things You have for me in response to my passionately fervent, extraordinary prayers."

As a starting point, I challenge you to give yourself to the pursuit of three things:

First, *read your Bible every day.* Absolutely nothing supersedes the daily consumption of God's Word. It is daily bread for your soul. Read it. Hide it in your heart. If you don't know where to start, ask God where He wants you to drop anchor, and leave your Bible open as you do a second thing.

Second, *read at least one segment daily.* Read it. Reflect upon it. Using the Prayer Response, pray it. Each segment takes about five minutes to read and reflect upon depending on how much time you take.

Third, *pray as you apply the principles in your life.* Do you worry too much or constantly ruminate about a crisis or pressing problem until it becomes almost unbearable? Do you try to sedate yourself by overeating? Christ's example of fasting *could* be key to the desperate help you need.

Each subtitle includes a Prayer Response that we can support in agreement, as mentioned in Matthew 18:19. This is not intended to cover all aspects of your prayers, but rather to serve as a prompt for prayer. Use the personalized prayer as a catalyst to explore new opportunities in your prayer life. I developed a deep appreciation for fasting late in my ministry. Like any other discipline, fasting should not be approached lightly or without careful consideration, as will be discussed further.

> **Prayer Response:** *"Be much in prayer and fasting, in secret and with one another. It seems to me, it would become the circumstances of the present day, if ministers would often meet, and spend days in fasting and fervent prayer, earnestly seeking those extraordinary supplies of Divine Grace... When God has something great to accomplish for His church, it is His will that there should precede it the extraordinary prayer of His people."*[3]
>
> —Jonathan Edwards

Nothing would thrill me more than for you to experience the miracle-working power of God in your life. New horizons of exceptional prayer await you. Let's get started.

---

[3] Jonathan Edwards, Thoughts on Revival, p. 209.

1

Refuse to Fly Solo

You might find yourself dedicating considerable time to prayer, whether kneeling or prostrate before God. This is perfectly fine. Exercise patience and trust that incredible outcomes will arise when you wait upon Him. Surrender to His will and collaborate with Him. Remember, you are aligning with His divine plan, not the other way around.

After successfully mobilizing two local churches for prayer, I was appointed to the office of District Superintendent (DS). I mistakenly believed that a praying pastor couldn't possibly transform into a praying superintendent capable of mobilizing an entire district to prayer. In my previous pastoral assignment, the Spirit had shown me that the church moves forward best on its knees, united in prayer. Consequently, I maintained a disciplined prayer life, both personally and privately.

After shouldering the burden of prayer largely by myself for many years, I heeded the Spirit's urging and started to gather Prayer Partners. My outlook transformed upon discovering John Mott's stirring challenge:

> "If added power accompanies the united prayer of two or three, imagine the tremendous victories that would occur when hundreds of thousands of faithful church members unite daily in prayer for the growth of Christ's Kingdom."[1]

It turned out that God had already been preparing a multitude of people to respond. I discovered that people will indeed pray if we simply ask them. God granted us nearly a thousand Prayer Partners from Northeast Texas.

God made us to be "fundamentally supernatural people," so we are called to pray and seek supernatural solutions. During the confinement of Covid, the book *Fearless Prayer* by Craig Hazen made a profound impact on me when he identified "the mother of all barriers" to prayer as naturalism—the belief that only physical or material things exist and that everything in the universe must be explained by science. In crisis situations, like when we dial 911 for expert medical help that is just minutes away, we often take for granted our access to immediate assistance. However, consider the people we know in Haiti or the rainforest of Guyana; when they cannot dial 911, they turn to prayer, relying on faith and the supernatural for support and intervention in their times of need.

> **Prayer Response:** *Heavenly Father, we come before You to ask for the grace to broaden our perspectives and expand our understanding. Help us to see beyond the limitations of our earthly experiences and to recognize how deeply interconnected we are as Your children in the supernatural realm. Teach us to embrace our shared identity in Christ and to support each other as we navigate the challenges of life, trusting in Your guidance and the profound connections that tie us together. Amen.*[2]

---

[1] John Mott quote found in AZ Quotes.
[2] Portions adapted from The De La Salle Brothers, "100 Prayers," 24.

Discover Strength in Shared Faith

Approach the throne of our gracious God with boldness and confidence, as encouraged in Hebrews 4:16. Remember that prayer is essential; without it, we miss out on daily blessings and the strength that fuels a powerful life.

After moving to Dallas to start my position as district superintendent, I had incorporated several key principles of prayer into my devotional routine. I was convinced that what worked in a local church setting could not be replicated across a district with many churches. Regrettably, I postponed embracing the need for prayer support. Reflecting on this delay, I hope it wasn't because I feared showing vulnerability, as suggested by one layman who questioned, "Why do you need more prayer? Can't you handle the pressure?"

Satan may have played a larger role in my procrastination than I care to admit, placing obstacles in my path that took months if not years to navigate. Yet, I discovered these hindrances can be surmounted. If you find yourself stuck behind an obstacle, muster your courage and take that initial step. The notion that no one will respond to your call for prayer is a lie from the devil. Overcome your reluctance.

Let nothing deter you from committing to the spiritual disciplines of prayer and fasting. Here's why: prayer is incredibly powerful. This isn't just a harmless ritual; there is raw power here. We have the privilege of accessing God Almighty if we choose to exercise it (Heb. 4:16). Overcome your doubts. Learn to pray. Mobilize God's people to pray. Refuse to navigate this journey alone and powerless. Work and wait in faith, believing, and you will witness God perform amazing deeds. There is miraculous power in prayer. Heather Riggleman aptly summarizes, "Who you become, the circumstances in your life, and the core of your character are all determined by what you talk to God about. According to the Bible, the power of prayer is, quite simply, the power of God, who hears and answers prayer."[3]

---

3 Heather Riggleman, Christianity.com, "What Is the Power of Prayer? April 21, 2020.

Inviting God into the work of our lives through prayer is a profound way to experience His supernatural presence and guidance in every aspect of our daily journey. When we entrust our decisions and paths to Him, we open ourselves to receiving the abundant graces that He is eager to bestow upon us. Whether it's strength to navigate challenges, wisdom to make the right choices, or peace to calm our worries, God is always ready to provide what we need. Prayer becomes a powerful connection between us and Him, nurturing our relationship and allowing His will to manifest in our lives. By consistently seeking His guidance and trusting in His plans, we find ourselves not only equipped to face each day with resilience but also enriched by the deep sense of purpose and fulfillment that comes from living in harmony with His will.

Prayer Response: *By the power of Jesus' name, I ask that You "set the fire down deep in my soul that I can't contain or control. There's no place I would rather be than here in your love… set a fire in my soul … I want more of You. Pour it out, Lord, pour it out. It's not how little but more and more and more. Pour it out, Jesus!"*[4]

Embrace the Power of Togetherness

The sincere prayers of a righteous individual hold tremendous power and yield wonderful results, as stated in James 5:16. When you devote yourself to prayer, it brings you closer to the Spirit, creating a reinforcing cycle where frequent prayer deepens your spiritual connection. This enhanced connection then encourages you to pray even more fervently.

While solitary prayer in your private prayer closet is powerful, do not feel constrained to that alone. Andrew Murray wisely advised, "It is in the closet, with the door shut, that the sound of abundance of rain will first be heard." Your prayers can transcend any geographical boundary and reach anywhere on this planet.

---

4 Inspired from "Set a fire down in my soul," by United Pursuit, Will Reagan.

Imagine the transformative power of a united force of prayer warriors, collectively invoking God's miraculous abilities as described in Matthew 18:19. Across the nation, God is summoning a group of spiritual arsonists to ignite revival fires far and wide. Perhaps God is calling you to broaden your prayer practices beyond personal communications with Him. Embrace the concept of collaboration and reject the idea of going it alone.

United prayer is faith in action. Many intercessors united through God's power could be the catalyst for a spiritual breakthrough in your church, community, and nation. When we tap into God's resources by faith and pray, things happen that often defy natural explanations. It is a privilege we must not relinquish. There is untapped strength and power in prayer that the Church has yet to fully realize. The approach is simple: experience the power of praying together.

Prayer Response: *Jesus, You promised, "Where two or three are gathered in My name, there am I among them" (Matt. 18:22, ESV). Yet, I rarely pray with other believers. Forgive me for often going solo in my prayer life. I trust that my prayers are heard. Now, please guide me to at least one other person to join with me in prayer, so that our collective power may be amplified, strength may counter my weakness, and Your presence unmistakable. In Your powerful name, Amen.*

Amplify the Power of Unified Prayer

The power of collective prayer and responsibility in faith can drive impactful change and spiritual awakening. In 2001, two esteemed Christian leaders from different generations and varied branches of Christianity united their efforts to challenge the Body of Christ to plant five million new churches for a Billion Soul Harvest. Today, the Billion Soul Network stands as the largest pastors' network in the world, representing more than 2,000 organizations and 500,000 churches globally.

Such an ambitious global effort demands a billion hours of prayer. Some reports suggest we are approaching a billion-soul harvest—"938,252,765 people saved. Second Billion®.5 million." Never underestimate the power of God's people when mobilized in unified prayer, especially when those prayers focus on the salvation of the lost. We cannot reach our fullest potential until we unite in prayer for those who are lost and dying. "Carpe diem." It's time to seize the day. Take full advantage of each day and the opportunities it brings as if they were your last. "Squeeze everything you can out of each day; don't waste a single moment because once it's gone, it can never be retrieved."[5] Waste no time praying whether it is God's will to save.

Engraved on a tombstone beneath a stone image of weeping angel in a Scottsville, TX, cemetery are these words: "If love couldst have saved thee, thou wouldst be saved." In other words, when we pray for the salvation and well-being of our loved ones and neighbors, we are aligning our desires with God's own wishes (Matt.18:14). God deeply cares for each person and desires their well-being and salvation even more than we can comprehend.

Prayer Response: *"Lord of the Harvest, we ask You to send laborers into the fields around the world. In every place where Your Word is preached, call and anoint fishers of men. Even in the most difficult places, let the nets be cast and filled with a new, abundant spiritual harvest. May the nets of salvation overflow with decisions for Christ in our homes, churches, schools, prisons, streets, cities, and nations. In Jesus' name. Amen."*[6]

The Perpetual Power of Prayer

When a church commits to intercession, it could catalyze a global movement, spreading the message of the Gospel more effectively. Unity and commitment to prayer strengthen a church's ability to ac-

---

5 Dennis Lee, "Seize every chance to serve God's purpose," The Spectrum, December 31, 2014.
6 Adapted "Pray the Lord of the Harvest to Send Laborers," Chavda Ministries. July 15, 2023.

complish its mission, promoting spiritual growth and transformation within communities.

God is more than willing to answer our selfless prayers for the salvation of our loved ones and friends, as stated in 2 Peter 3:9. Although the answers to our prayers may seem slow in coming, making us wonder if we will ever live to see them fulfilled, we must hold firmly to the promise: "The Lord isn't slow to keep His promise…" from His perspective. From our viewpoint, however, it is a different story. Honestly, I pray that some of my closest companions will live to witness the salvation of their sons and daughters. Some of us have been waiting for years, while others have passed away without seeing their prayers answered.

Our prayers are eternally significant. Even when those who prayed have passed, their prayers remain forever before God, transcending their lives and enduring through generations and beyond.

No prayer is in vain. The enduring prayers of the saints will ultimately be answered. Prayer not only opens doors and amplifies efforts but also prepares the way for divine action and human response, just as someone's prayer opened Lydia's heart in Acts 16:14-15. Keep believing; our prayers persist and pave the way.

God calls us to reach those unreached around our churches, and united prayer is our powerful tool, breaking chains and opening doors. Praying together strengthens our collective faith and authority, replacing our doubts and fears with peace and confidence. This communal prayer taps into divine strength, uplifting us and equipping us to face challenges. Together, we gain the courage and clarity to overcome darkness and negativity. This reinforces prayer's crucial role in our spiritual practices, fostering resilience and unity as we confront life's trials.

Prayer Response: *Father, please fulfill our prayers for unsaved loved ones and friends (name them), guarding their steps with Your goodness and love. May Your grace* *lead them to salvation. Open their ears to hear Your voice and see their need for You. IN Jesus' name, Amen.*

Urgency and Desperation

In John 4:35, Jesus urgently calls us to recognize that the fields are already ripe for harvest, signaling an immediate need to spread the Gospel and transform lives. P. Douglas Small highlights how the church's significant progress is always enveloped in fervent prayer and deep devotion. These insights urgently remind believers that now is the critical time for spiritual action, and that intense prayer is both the driving force behind, and a marker of, effective missionary work. By embracing this desperate need and dedicating ourselves to prayer, the church can propel God's kingdom forward and ignite a profound spiritual revival.

A global harvest, an answer to the prayers of our forebears, has been underway for some time. The Asbury Revival of 2023 began among Generation Z but also attracted many older saints who witnessed firsthand the outpouring they had long prayed for. We are standing on the shoulders of many devoted individuals to receive this blessing.

The last century, particularly the past two decades, marks perhaps the most fruitful era for the Church to date. Since 1900, seventy percent of all conversions since 100 A.D. have occurred, with the majority of these happening post-World War II. Notably, seventy percent of these recent convert s were reached following the inception of the "Praying through the Window" initiative, highlighting a significant surge in effective evangelism.

Since the first "Walk thru the Window" in 1992, an astonishing 30 percent of all conversions since 100 A.D. have occurred, matching the number reached in the initial eighteen centuries—in less than two decades. This means that the church's growth rate over the past 20 years has been 180 times faster than in previous centuries, 26 times the rate of the 20th century. We are indeed living in a remarkable era of unprecedented spiritual harvest. Truly, God is on the move.[7]

---
7 P. Douglas Small, "God is At Work," blog, February 23, 2017, cited from DAWN.

The recent baptism of 4,166 individuals at Pirate Cove Beach on Pentecost Sunday underscores the readiness of North America's spiritual harvest. With seven percent of the unchurched already looking to visit a church and another 33 percent open to discussing faith, the potential for growth is significant. However, the trend of Christians viewing evangelism as optional is concerning. When was the last time you engaged in a conversation about God? This moment invites reflection on our role in extending invitations to explore faith.[8] It's time to overcome our hesitations and embrace the opportunity to engage more deeply in matters of faith.

Prayer Response: *Lord of the harvest, we humbly ask that You guide us to every place You want us to go. Use us to both preach and demonstrate the good news of Your Kingdom. Help us to bring others along on this journey, equipping them to engage in the exciting work of the Gospel. Lord, let us witness people's lives being transformed by the incredible grace of Christ. We earnestly desire to see more and more of this transformative impact in our town. Amen.[9] In the Mighty Name of Jesus, Amen.*

Fulfill God's Purpose

Exodus 17:12 captures a poignant scene of support and perseverance, where Aaron and Hur hold up Moses' hands, securing victory in battle. This reflects how collective effort strengthens leadership and achieves divine purposes. Prayer is pivotal in propelling God's work, acting as the bedrock that sustains His mission. This narrative underlines the essential link between human collaboration and divine intervention, reminding believers of the importance of continuous prayer and communal support in fulfilling God's plans and securing spiritual triumphs.

The supernatural is unleashed when believers come together in earnest prayer, approaching God with open hearts and a spirit of humility.

---

8 Barna, "Sharing Faith Is Increasingly Optional to Christians," May 15, 2018.
9 Adapted from Scott Pauley, "5 Prayers of the Evangelist," Enjoying the Journey website.

This unity and reverence create a space for divine intervention, allowing God's transformative power to work in individuals, communities, and the world at large. In this atmosphere of faith and surrender, miracles can manifest, and lives transformed.

Why then do we hesitate to rally people for fervent prayer? Calling your church to pray can be challenging but calling an entire district of over sixty churches—ranging from small to large and everything in between—to a united prayer effort is another level of daunting. Yet, God always has men and women of prayer ready to respond. Before long, the number of prayer partners can soar to nearly a thousand.

The loneliness of leadership is a well-known phenomenon. Many of us are all too familiar with the isolation that comes when crises arise, or when we must make solo decisions that carry significant weight. It becomes particularly challenging when you can't openly discuss or explain the situation. Choosing to carry the burden of leadership alone is a lonesome decision. While confidentiality may prevent a leader from disclosing everything, relationships can still be cultivated with people who pray. Foster these prayer connections. You don't have to carry the burden alone; leaders don't have to fly solo.

God has a team, like Aaron and Hur, ready to support through intercession—leaders simply need to ask. Facing fatigue, loneliness, and the burden of responsibility, leaders can greatly benefit from prayer partners. By mutually uplifting each other in prayer, a network of spiritual support forms, helping sustain leaders through tough times. Victory, as seen when Moses was supported, can likewise be found by modern leaders through intercessory prayers. This cooperation not only strengthens leaders but also emphasizes the power of communal faith in overcoming obstacles and reaching goals.

Prayer Response: *God, I pray that You would bless our leaders with Your divine wisdom and the mind of Christ, enabling them to make decisions with deep understanding and humility. Surround them with godly counsel and advisors who intimately know You and walk faithful-*

ly in Your ways. Guide our leaders as You see fit. We pray that they would yield to Your Spirit and embrace Your wisdom. Lead them according to Your perfect will and help them fulfill their God-given destinies and accomplish the assignments You have set before them. Amen[10]

Communicate, Communicate, Communicate!

Our prayers often lack the specificity that can make them truly fervent and effective (James 5:16). Just as we are specific in our praises, we should approach prayer with the same level of intentionality and thankfulness. Focused and passionate prayer not only invites divine intervention but also fosters a spirit of gratitude for the exact ways God answers. By praying with purpose and clarity, we are better positioned to recognize and celebrate the specific manifestations of God's grace in our lives.

Information serves as the fuel for the fire of prayer. Effective communication is essential when people enthusiastically respond to prayer mobilization efforts. Well-informed intercessors become intelligent intercessors, achieving greater effectiveness when a structured approach to prayer is provided. Without a well-defined prayer plan, we often resort to vague and general petitions better know our "Bless and be With" prayers. Specific, sincere, and faith-filled prayers are both powerful and effective.

Never assume that everyone who responds to a call for prayer knows how to pray effectively. Respondents can be instructed in how to offer specific prayers. Serious intercession—prayer that is truly impactful—requires us to move beyond general, vague petitions. We need to go further than simply asking God to "bless" and "be with" those we are praying for, as such requests can sometimes become empty phrases devoid of depth. Instead, our prayers must be specific, heartfelt, and purposeful. We should seek to understand the needs and struggles of those we lift up, asking God for tangible miracles, healing, guidance,

---

10 Adapted from Pastoral Care Team, "8 Prayers for Your Leaders," K-Love, March 15, 2023.

and transformation. Engaging earnestly and intentionally in prayer invites the Holy Spirit to move powerfully in their lives. This approach deepens our connection with God and fosters genuine compassion for others, making our supplications more aligned with His will and purpose.

There are several ways to communicate regularly with prayer partners, such as group texts or emails for instant updates. Direct, personal communication is crucial when enlisting someone for prayer, ensuring they are provided with accurate, specific information. Clearly defined, focused prayers help deepen engagement with our intentions, align our hearts with God's will, and enhance mental clarity to better understand our needs and desired outcomes. Furthermore, these precise prayers bolster our faith by requiring intentional thought about what we are asking for.

Praying with a kingdom focus ensures that our prayers are not just about personal gain but are aligned with the broader purposes of God's work in the world. By doing so, we cultivate a prayer life that seeks not only personal transformation but also the advancement of God's kingdom on earth.

Approaching prayer with confidence stems from trust in God's power and promises. By being specific and intentional, we present our requests with the assurance that God is attentive to our prayers and capable of acting in mighty ways. Such prayers, rooted in faith and clarity, can indeed be powerful and effective. Jessie Synan explains that brief, spontaneous prayers can alter our mindset and perspective. They have the power to re-orient us, but only if they are expressed as abruptly as the thought itself.[11]

Prayer Response: *Father God, appoint new intercessors with a holy desperation for prayer. Let them see Your*

---

[11] Jessie Synan, Pray With Confidence, "An Incredibly Short Prayer For Focus [& 12 Other Example Prayers]."

promises fulfilled and witness great and mighty things beyond our understanding. Awaken Your church to embrace new mantles of prayer and respond to Your call with specific, focused intercession. By the Spirit of Christ Jesus, who lives to intercede, instill in every believer the spirit of unceasing prayer as commanded in Your Word. Amen.[12] *In Jesus' holy name. Amen.*

Persistence Pays

Indeed, persistent and evolving communication with God through daily and continuous prayer is essential for effectively navigating life's ever-changing landscape. Rather than clinging to outdated practices, engaging in ongoing, discerning prayer allows us to remain adaptable and responsive to new challenges and opportunities. This type of prayer promotes a dynamic relationship with God, where constant dialogue helps in seeking clarity and understanding the divine will. As circumstances change, this practice equips us with the spiritual insight needed to make wise decisions that align with our faith and God's plan for our lives. Thus, continuous prayer is not just a ritual, but a vital tool for personal growth and spiritual resilience.

Kennon Callahan spoke to a group of leaders about "the future that has come." He cautioned us against urging people to make long-term, year-round commitments, as very few can sustain more than one such commitment, like attending church every Sunday. I broke Callahan's rule when I asked for an open-ended commitment to prayer. Intercessory prayer, after all, is not for "excellent sprinters," but for "solid marathon runners." Clearly, I wasn't among the men of Issachar who understood "the cultural paradigm shift" taking place.

Though I may not possess Issachar-like wisdom, we've collectively realized the transformative power of prayer. Mark Batterson notes in *Whisper* that intercessors are those who listen to God for others. One intercessor, sensing my challenging week, affirmed, "The Lord told me." In times of uncertainty, be it illness or any heartbreak, it's crucial

---
12 The Father's Business, "Pray For God To Call Out Intercessors," September 12, 2012.

to find someone connected deeply with God—someone who, as Spurgeon suggested, might "mention your name" in their prayers. Quonda Renee emphasizes the vital role of intercessory prayer as a spiritual practice that bridges gaps through expressions of love, empathy, and concern. It enables believers to impact the world meaningfully, often from afar. Renee's mantra to "own it, use it, it works" speaks to the powerful, albeit sometimes subtle, effects of prayer in bringing peace, guidance, and transformative change.[13]

> **Prayer Response:** *God, today I pray for someone (name them) who is feeling weak right now. May they experience the transformative power of Your presence, lifting them from their troubles and weakness to a place of strength that You have ordained, far above hurts, harm, and the threats and injuries of this evil world. Let Your presence strengthen their body, soul, and spirit, heal their emotions, fortify their will, and lead them to experience Your ultimate joy and strength today. In Jesus' name. Amen.*

The Necessity of Repentance

Repentance is an opportunity for us to renew our commitment to our faith and realign our actions with God's will, welcoming us back into a life that reflects His plans for us. Similarly, dedicating ourselves to praying selflessly for others is one of the highest callings we can embrace. It reflects the profound, Christlike act of intercession where we put the needs of others before our own. By listening to divine guidance and practicing heartfelt, compassionate prayer, we are invited to engage in a life of active faith that blends obedience with a genuine care for those around us—a testament to both our spiritual growth and our commitment to nurturing the community.

Haggai the prophet heard God's voice and boldly relayed His message to the people, as told in Haggai 1. The people had prioritized their

---

[13] Adapted from Quonda Renee, "10 Intercessory Prayers," I Need a Word.

luxurious homes over rebuilding the Temple, prompting God to raise a messenger to spur them into action. Acting as God's mouthpiece, Haggai delivered God's word, not his own. Theologians often ponder, "Who speaks for God?" and highlight the Bible as the ultimate authority—Sola Scriptura. I wholeheartedly affirm that the Bible is the authoritative Word of God and that prophets act as His spokesmen; their duty is to convey God's revelation, not their personal views.

Those tasked with conveying God's Word should do so truthfully, lovingly, and faithfully, allowing the outcomes to be determined by His will. Once directed by Him, our role is merely to pass on His message to the people and leave the results in His hands. By embracing this approach, we maintain a clear conduit for His truths, ensuring that our actions and words align with His plans and not our own.

When an army of nearly a thousand intercessors was enlisted from across the Dallas District, we convened for a first-ever Prayer Summit, not fully aware of the far-reaching effects such united prayer would produce (Eph. 3:20). Understanding that we lead by example, pastors and leaders gathered in Jesus' name to hear what God might say. Our spiritual leaders consecrated themselves, and "the repenters" repented. We asked the Holy Spirit to purge us of anything offensive to God (2 Chronicles 29:5). Not every pastor participated; only those who could and would obey the call to prayer (29:15).

Refuse to get bogged down by the percentage of participants. We don't need ninety to a hundred percent participation. A reasonable goal is ten percent of our people willing to humble themselves, pray, and seek God's face. Spiritual renewal must begin with the leaders. We should take courage and exercise faith, for God will strengthen and help us. The Lord will uphold us with His righteous hand. Prayerful leaders are effective leaders. As leaders, our actions speak volumes. We should dedicate time each day to prayer and reflection, showing our community or organization the importance we place on seeking divine guidance.

To foster a culture where prayer is integral, both in personal practices and in group gatherings, consider initiating weekly prayer meetings or special events focused on spiritual growth and intercession. Inspiring those around you to exercise faith, especially in challenging times, is crucial. Affirm that while obstacles may seem daunting, faith and prayer provide strength, comfort, and solutions.

By promoting an environment where prayer and spiritual seeking are prioritized, leaders can effectively guide their communities toward renewal and transformation, grounded in faith and mutual support. This approach not only enhances the spiritual vitality of the group but also strengthens the communal bonds, creating a supportive network that thrives on faith and collective resilience.

Prayer Response: *Oh Lord, Your Word declares that You are our Good Shepherd. Just as shepherds provide guidance for their sheep, we pray that You, Lord, will provide guidance for every leader. I pray that You help them (insert names here) to be more like You, and especially to be an example in prayer. Help them know the condition of their flock. I pray that every leader will give careful attention those they lead, and that the relationship between those they lead will flourish. This is the prayer of our heart. Amen.*[14]

The Path to Revival

We must challenge ourselves to continually grow and adapt, not only embracing change as it comes but also actively seeking improvement in all areas of our lives. This pursuit requires honesty, resilience, and the willingness to step outside our comfort zones. By tackling each challenge head-on, we can unlock new opportunities for personal development and contribute positively to the communities around us. Remember, progress is often born out of adversity, and by embracing the challenges we face, we pave the way for a brighter, more robust future.

---

[14] Adapted from ConnectUS, "6 Good Prayers for Leadership Guidance," June 3, 2019.

Throughout Scripture and history, God has used prophets and prophetic voices to call His people back to the altar for its repair, to repentance, and to prayer. Sadly, when prophets are ignored, the people suffer. Those who inspire God's people to pray for revival are rare. The awakening we need and profess to desire requires fervent prayer. If you are indifferent to prayer and revival, your people will be indifferent as well. Leonard Ravenhill noted, "The person who can get believers to praying would, under God, usher in the greatest revival of holiness that the world has ever known."

Unanswered prayer can result from unconfessed sin (Psalm 66:18). To foster a right relationship with God, repentance is crucial as it clears the path for our prayers to be heard. Effective prayer necessitates soul-searching, confession, and genuine repentance, especially during Prayer Summits. The Holy Spirit often reveals shortcomings that must be openly confessed and repented to maintain a prayerful condition. Being right with God involves confession and full commitment to Christ, the only solution for sin removal. Revival stagnates without addressing sin with humility and honest self-examination.

Stephen and Alex Kendrick highlight the critical importance of sincerity and repentance in prayer, emphasizing that God doesn't respond to deceitful or empty cries. They remind us that God directs how prayer works, not us, and caution against certain "Locks of Prayer" that can restrict its effectiveness. Chief among these is praying from an unrepentant heart, which can hinder our prayers and diminish their impact, ultimately causing us to undermine our own spiritual efforts.[15]

Prayer Response: *Dear Lord, I am deeply grateful for the grace You have bestowed upon me, allowing me to repent. You have promised to listen to me from heaven and grant the desires of my heart. Please change my heart, O God. Transform me through the renewal of my mind so that I may no longer conform to the ways of this world. I repent of all the things that have hindered my prayers,*

---
15 Stephen and Alex Kendrick, The Battle Plan of Prayer," (Nashville: B&H Publishing, 2015.

and I release anything that might prevent my prayers from being answered. Cleanse me with Your blood and make me pure. Amen.[16]

Spiritual Health Check

I find great comfort in knowing that, just like in Psalm 66:19, God listens to my prayers and showers me with love. This assurance encourages me to pray confidently, as Whitney Hopler suggests, bringing a transformative peace to my spiritual journey.

Just as I routinely visit Dr. Mousakis for thorough skin check-ups, ensuring I stay on top of any potential health issues from my sun-filled Florida childhood, I also tend to my spiritual well-being with regular prayer and reflection. The process may be uncomfortable at times—like the sting of cryotherapy—but it's a crucial step in nurturing peace of mind and fostering a deeper connection with the Almighty.

Let's allow the Great Physician to examine us today and reveal any problem areas that need attention (Ps. 139:24). When He points out an issue, make no excuses; instead, cry out (confess) and ask for the cleansing blood of Jesus to be applied, as it continually purifies us from all sin (1 John 1:7). His diagnosis should inspire an urgency to maintain a clean heart and hands (Ps. 24:7). Don't dismiss something as insignificant when God says it's crucial. Remember, Satan may downplay it, but he's a liar. Watchman Nee wisely advised, "People who cover their faults and excuse themselves do not have a repentant spirit."

In 2 Chronicles 29, Hezekiah ordered the priests to reopen the temple, but they first had to remove the trash. The idols, pagan altars and symbols, and all the accumulated rubbish and filth had to go. It took eight days to clear all the debris (2 Chron. 29:18-19). When leaders are cleansed and renewed, they become catalysts for prayer and renewal within their sphere of influence. "Prayer catalysts are always thinking about ways to engage more people in prayer," clarifies Carol Madison. "They champion prayer, show up for prayer, and invite others to join them on prayer adventures."[17]

---

16 Adapted from Prayray.com, "Prayer for Repentance and Cleansing," July 16, 2023.
17 Carol Madison, Pray Beyond Blog, "Prayer Leader or Prayer Catalyst."

Corporate prayer gatherings offer a vital opportunity for communal acknowledgment and forgiveness of sins, laying a foundation for confident and effective prayer, as suggested in Psalm 66:18. By confessing and turning from past ways, we start to bear the fruits of repentance (Matthew 3:8), thus welcoming a renewed outpouring of God's Spirit. This revitalization can cure spiritual lukewarmness, impotence, and powerlessness, leading to dynamic transformation within our churches. However, for such renewal to take place, it is crucial for God to first awaken our cold hearts, reigniting our fervor and commitment.

> **Prayer Response:** *Lord, guide me to quiet my mind before You, allowing You to search my heart and reflect on my actions. Through Your Holy Spirit, reveal to me any shortcomings in my life (name any the Spirit reveals). I acknowledge that, in my own strength, my efforts to change are in vain. Please help me to surrender complete control of my life into Your hands. Forgive me for ever thinking, "I'm better than most." May Your Word serve as the mirror that reveals my true self. I desire to see myself as You do, through the lens of truth. "Cleanse me, purify me... I long for the double cure!" Amen.*

The Power of Corporate Confession

In Nehemiah 1:6, the earnest plea for God to listen as he confesses his and his people's sins resonates deeply with me. It's a reminder that I, too, must acknowledge not just my personal shortcomings but also the broader, collective failings we are all part of. Anderson and Mylander in their book *Setting Your Church Free* suggest that corporate sins and associated shame are not limited to Bible times. We must seek forgiveness and strive for change within our family and community. We must approach prayer with humility and sincere hearts, asking for guidance and strength to confront shared challenges, while believing in the possibility of redemption and transformation for us all.

Nehemiah's prayer serves as a potent example of corporate confession—an all-encompassing act of repentance. I once tended to avoid it, but I now recognize the essential role of corporate repentance. "Corporate repentance is a unified prayer by the people of God, confessing the sins of family, church, or nation that the Spirit has revealed."[18] The cultural reformation we need must begin with godly leaders seeking the Lord. Now, more than ever, our land requires a culture-reshaping revival.

Confessing corporate sins holds significant power; it removes the hindrances to prayer and sets us on firm praying ground. We must allow the Holy Spirit to identify the obstacles that block our access to grace through repentance. Vance Havner once remarked, "Most church members live so far below the standard, you would have to backslide to be in fellowship with them." Unconfessed sin hinders prayer, and the Lord will not hear us unless we repent and turn from our wicked ways.

In *Setting Your Church Free,* Anderson and Mylander warn that the issue of corporate sins and associated shame persists in modern congregations, potentially including yours, where entire churches or significant groups within may fall into wrong patterns. To heal and prevent further damage within ourselves and our churches, it's crucial to repent of these tolerated sinful behaviors, eliminating any practices that displease God. The church needs to address its internal problems first to restore its influence on the world, by acknowledging that minimizing or mislabeling sins as mere mistakes undermines true spiritual integrity. As P. Douglas Small emphasizes, "Sin is not just a minor error; it is deadly!" The misuse of grace in contemporary churches, where it becomes a license for negligence toward sin, highlights the urgent need for genuine repentance and profound transformation.

> **Prayer Response:** *Heavenly Father, we seek Your forgiveness for our sins. Pardon both the transgressions we remember and those we have forgotten. Forgive us for our numerous shortcomings when faced with temptation*

---

18 Salem Alliance.org, "A Biblical Case for Spirit-Prompted Corporate Repentance."

and for our stubbornness in resisting correction. We ask for forgiveness for the harsh judgments we have cast upon others, as well as the leniency we have afforded ourselves. Forgive us for the lies we have told and the truths we have evaded. Pardon the pain we have inflicted on others and the self-indulgence we have allowed ourselves. Lord God, have mercy on us and make us whole. In the name of Jesus Christ, our Savior, we pray. Amen.[19]

The Danger of Superficial Repentance

Hosea 5:6 is a sobering reminder that outward rituals and sacrifices are not enough if our hearts are distant from God. It highlights the importance of genuine humility and contrition in our spiritual walk. Despite God's majesty and holiness, His true fellowship is with those who are humble and contrite in spirit, seeking Him sincerely. Even when God's anger and accusations manifest due to our failings, His grace assures us that they do not endure indefinitely. His unfailing compassion invites us back into relationship with Him, encouraging us to approach Him with honest hearts and a willingness to change. It's this grace that transforms our lives, fostering a deeper, more authentic connection with God.

Can you imagine going to God to apologize for your sin with every intention of committing it again? This is exactly what Israel did during Hosea's time. They offered "superficial repentance," bringing their flocks and herds to make a general apology, but their lives never changed. Christine Wyrtzen describes this accurately—it is superficial, not true repentance. Such insincere repentance—repentance that is as vague as our sin—is not taken seriously by God. "It's as if He sees us coming with all our pretentiousness and closes His eyes in dread at the meaningless babbling that follows."[20] Words are meaningless if our actions don't support them. When we say "I'm sorry" without sincerity, we belittle the sacrifice of the Lamb of God on the Cross. Genuine

---
19 Adapted from Wayside Presbyterian Church, "Prayers of Confession."
20 Christine Wyrtzen, "Superficial Repentance," Daughters of Promise, September 11, 2021.

revival demands that people change their actions, attitudes, behaviors, addictions, and anything else that hinders their walk with Christ. Otherwise, it becomes what Milton Quintanilla describes as "superficial repentance," characterized by "empty words" or "mere virtue signaling without any practical impact."[21]

Genuine repentance requires a complete U-turn from a diluted, unbiblical Gospel that may offer emotional satisfaction but fails to bring about true-life transformation. The comprehensive truth of the Gospel must be proclaimed with renewed holy boldness, addressing the diluted versions that have led to the acceptance of false doctrines. If we have compromised our Christian convictions by embracing a watered-down Gospel, repentance is essential. T.M. Moore wisely states, "When it comes to sin, let's not mince words, and let's not act like it's not the big deal it is. No progress in faith can be made where sin is not consistently and thoroughly confessed, repented of, and forsaken." Superficial repentance will not suffice; deep, sincere transformation is necessary to align with God's truth. This means confronting and correcting the ways we have strayed from the core tenets of our faith, ensuring our beliefs and actions reflect the undiluted power of the Gospel.

> **Prayer Response:** *Dear God, I humbly come before You to repent and turn away from my sin. Jesus, thank You for dying on the cross so that I can be reconciled with the Father and be set free from the bondage of sin. Please forgive me for those times when I had the best of intentions but still repeated the sins for which I had already sought forgiveness. Grant me the power of Your Spirit to keep me from stumbling. Give me clean hands and a pure heart. "Wash me, and I shall be whiter than snow..." Sanctify me thoroughly. In the only name by which I must be saved, Jesus, Amen.*

---

21 Milton Quantanilla, "10 Things the Church Must Repent of Today," Crosswalk.com, January 24, 2023.

Apostolic Boldness and Transformation

The courage of the apostles as portrayed in the Acts of the Apostles is striking. After praying for boldness (Acts 4:31), they were filled with the Holy Spirit and fearlessly preached the Gospel, proclaiming the risen Christ. Amidst these events, a subtler but profound transformation occurred among the believers and their community, characterized by love, truth, and spiritual unity—an equally significant miracle.

In today's context, particularly in the wake of the pandemic, this kind of transformation remains crucial. The church today needs a revival that not only brings us closer to Christ-like behavior but also enriches our lives with the fruits of the Spirit while maintaining a strong adherence to truth. Those open to God's influence in their lives will experience profound changes—they will be touched, healed, taught, inspired, and transformed to embody more of Christ's attributes.

If America is going to repent of its many sins, it must first witness the church repenting of its own. As 1 Peter 4:17-18 reminds us, judgment begins at the house of the Lord. This means that the transformation must start within the church, setting an example for the rest of society. When our worldly friends observe our sincere repentance, even for our smallest transgressions (if there is such a thing), they might recognize their own need for change. Seeing our genuine remorse may lead them to think, "If they see the need to repent, perhaps I need to make significant changes in my life as well."[22]

In the light of God's holiness, our righteousness often seems inadequate. Holy people are humble people, acknowledging their own shortcomings and striving for greater alignment with God's will. Prayer plays a crucial role in this process, as focused, intense, and breakthrough prayer is essential if we hope to witness miracles and transformations, both in our lives and in the broader world. Such prayer not only brings us closer to God but also empowers us to effect change and demonstrate His love and truth to others.

---

22 Quotations from P. Douglas Small, Prayer—The Heart of It All (Kannapolis: Alive Publications, 2018) 158-159.

Prayer Response: *Lord Jesus, I humbly pray that You envelop me with Your Holy Spirit. Draw me into a deeper faith in You, for You are capable of all things. In accordance with Your eternal mercy, establish, strengthen, and reconcile me in Christ. Transform me, allowing me to focus my mind on things above rather than on earthly matters. As I study Your Word, renew my heart by transforming my mind (Romans 12:1), so that I may engage with this world—one You have not abandoned—with integrity and holiness. May my life bear an abundance of lasting, spiritual fruit (John 15:1-5). Grant me the grace and wisdom to represent You well, so that glory may be given to our Father in heaven and the Kingdom of Christ our Lord may be advanced. Amen.*

2

Unleashing the Supernatural

"Impossible odds set the stage for God's greatest miracles!"
—Mark Batterson

If Spirit-filled believers are inherently supernatural individuals, what prevents us from witnessing miracles regularly? Craig Hazen argues in *Fearless Prayer* that we have been profoundly influenced by naturalism, which he calls the "mother of all barriers" to prayer, resulting in our almost complete "de-supernaturalization." We have been immersed in the "bitter marinade" of naturalism for so long that when God answers prayers, we often dismiss it as a coincidence, failing to recognize that every answered prayer is a miracle.

Do not deceive yourself: if you pray, it is a testament to the presence of faith within you. Conversely, a lack of prayer often signifies an absence of faith. However, when you engage in prayer, do so with the full expectation that the God of miracles will reveal Himself. Throughout history, God has consistently displayed His power in spectacular and awe-inspiring ways. This assurance should fuel our prayers, encouraging us to approach Him with confidence and anticipation.

When we pray with expectation, we align ourselves with the biblical narrative of a God who intervenes, who listens, and who acts. Whether in grand, miraculous events or in the quiet transformations of the heart, His power is boundless. Our task is to approach Him with a heart full of faith, trusting not only in His ability to act but also in His wisdom to do what is best. This posture of prayer not only strengthens our relationship with God but also opens avenues for His power to manifest in ways beyond our imagination.

> **Prayer Response:** *"Dearest Jesus, please help me. I come to You, my Creator of miracles, in my time of need. Although I know You are always with me, these times feel particularly dark, and I need You now more than ever. You are my light in the darkness, and I know that I can only rise again with You by my side. Amen."*[23]

United Prayer Yields Miraculous Results

If we gather to pray, invoking the presence of Christ in all our endeavors, we may expect phenomenal results. After our initial Prayer Summit, we, both pastors and laypeople, spread throughout Northeastern Texas with a resolve to become praying churches, consistently invoking the presence of Christ. Our united prayer began to yield miraculous results.

With the growth of the Hispanic population in NE Texas, we began praying for opportunities to connect with them for Christ. This prayer expanded our vision, and God began to inspire us to reach souls within the burgeoning Hispanic community in Tyler, Texas. Abiel Hernandez was appointed as our Hispanic Coordinator. He mobilized Hispanic leaders, and together we started envisioning places for new

---
23 Daniel Gallik, "Miracle Prayer: 10 Prayers For The Impossible," Christian Resources, May 21, 2024.

churches to be planted. United prayer should focus on Kingdom purposes. Miracles happen. Mountains move. Revival comes. Communities are transformed. The course of nations changes. Extraordinary prayer yields supernatural results. As Frederick Buechner elucidates, "A miracle is when the whole is greater than the sum of its parts. A miracle is when one plus one equals a thousand."

The ultimate purpose of prayer is communion with God, while its noblest characteristic lies in intercession, especially when we pray fervently for lost and broken people. Moving beyond safe and comfortable prayers, we are called to engage in what are often termed "dangerous prayers," focusing on matters that deeply grieve God's heart. Dale Reeves eloquently points out that this approach is radically different from the convenient, self-focused prayers typical in modern, popularized Christianity. By embracing audacious prayers that ask God to align our hearts with His concerns, we open ourselves to the possibility of witnessing profound miracles. This shift requires courage and vulnerability but promises a deeper connection with God's transformative power and purpose.[24]

Prayer Response: *"Lord, break my heart today with the things that break Yours." When our hearts break for what breaks Yours, we become aware of the limitations inherent in our human nature, contrasted with the boundlessness of Your character. Your redemptive power transforms even the most painful circumstances, finding ways to reassemble every broken piece to fulfill Your purposes. In both words and actions, may we not only feel the breaking but also embrace the responsibility to rebuild with greater fervor, stronger faith, and hearts fully united in the pursuit of God's truth.[25] In Jesus's name. Amen.*

---

[24] Dale Reeves, Christ's Church, "Things That Break God's Heart."
[25] Adapted from Kaitlyn Parker, "Break My Heart for What Breaks Yours," The Lifestyle Journal.

Street Ministry Miracles

In April 1998, after weeks of prayer and seeking God's guidance, it was time to act. The Spirit led Abiel Hernandez, our Hispanic Coordinator, to Tyler, Texas, to conduct ten days of street meetings in the heart of the Hispanic community. While following God's guidance does not promise an easy path, it often leads to miracles for those who obey. Pastor Abiel loaded a rickety old church bus with over forty enthusiastic people who all shared a passion for serving the Spanish-speaking population in Tyler.[26]

For weeks, Abiel had been tirelessly embarking on the three-hour journey from Dallas to Tyler, fueled by a vision of establishing a vibrant place of worship for the Hispanic community. Despite the setbacks, his determination never wavered. Every trip seemed to end in disappointment, with numerous vacant properties but none were available for a meeting place. Property owners were either unresponsive or unwilling to accommodate Abiel's requests, leaving him frustrated but undeterred.

Undaunted by these challenges, Abiel's resolve only grew stronger. He knew the importance of community and the transformative power of faith. So, he pressed forward with plans for the launch service, rallying the support and enthusiasm of those who believed in this mission. On the day of the service, Abiel loaded the bus with hopeful and eager individuals, each one filled with anticipation for what this new beginning could mean.

As they traveled to Tyler, the bus resonated with excitement and possibility. They all knew that the journey was not only about a physical destination but about creating a spiritual home that would serve as a beacon of hope and fellowship. Even without a permanent building, the spirit of the community was already forming, bound together by shared faith and vision. Abiel was ready to embrace whatever came

---

[26] The source of this story is credited to Joyce Williams and an article entitled, "Heavenly Connections," and is used with permission.

next, knowing that with perseverance and faith, the right doors would eventually open.

Prayer Response: *Lord, today I pray for a renewed vision of Your plans for me and the grace to follow Your guidance. Sometimes I wish for a clear sign, like a blinking neon light or a guiding cloud, to affirm Your will in the decisions I make. However, it is truly Your presence that I seek. Help me find peace in knowing that You are always with me. If I stumble or stray, I trust that You will lead me back to Your path. Heavenly Father, please forgive me for rushing ahead of Your plans. Teach me to pause and listen for Your direction. Amen.*[27] *In Jesus' Name. Amen.*

A Meeting Place Without Walls

As Abiel saw the city limits sign for Tyler that evening, he recalled his prayer walk through the neighborhood and the grassy knoll where he had envisioned "a meeting place without walls." He directed the driver to head towards the town square. The bus turned into an alley, and Abiel whispered a quick prayer. The driver parked the bus behind three trees bordering a verdant plaza.

Before anyone got off the bus, Abiel stood at the front to give instructions. "There's something I need to tell you before we disembark," he said, somewhat sheepishly. "We couldn't secure the building, but God has given us this spot for our service tonight." He pushed the door open and led his group of devoted workers off the bus. Without a single word of complaint or dismay, everyone followed their visionary leader. "It's good to pray and wait when a situation isn't clear," advises Barbara Harper. "But when a change in plans is obviously from God, we need to accept it."[28]

---

27 Gleaned from "15 Prayers for Guidance and Wisdom When You Need Direction from God," Crosswalk.com, January 31, 2023.
28 Barbara Harper, Stray Thoughts, "When God Changes Your Plans," January 4, 2022.

The scent of freshly mowed grass greeted them as they began to unload the sound equipment and set up the chairs in the open air. The entire environment seemed vibrant and untouched, as if it had been prepared just for this occasion. As Abiel surveyed the scene, a wave of emotion overtook him, and tears began to moisten his eyes. In that moment, he realized that the Lord had been preparing their sanctuary all along, even down to the meticulous care of nature's "carpeting."

Abiel felt a profound sense of peace as he understood that the greatest blessings often come from surrendering our plans and trusting in a higher purpose. This unexpected change in venue did not deter them, but rather added a layer of authenticity and resilience to their gathering. It was a powerful reminder that while Plan A might not always unfold as expected, there's often a greater plan at work, shaped by faith and adaptability.

With this newfound perspective, Abiel and those with him embraced the moment. The location, though different from what they had initially imagined, was perfect in its simplicity and beauty. The community came together, drawn by the spirit of unity and hope that filled the air. By staying flexible and open to possibilities, everything worked out remarkably well. What had begun as a challenge transformed into a testament to faith's power in the face of uncertainty, setting the stage for a meaningful and memorable gathering.

Prayer Response: *"Father, I am seeking. Though I feel hesitant and uncertain, I ask You, O God, to watch over each step I take and guide me along the way" (Augustine). I submit myself to You, trusting that You will direct my paths. I have confidence that Your guidance is always the best route to follow. I pray that You create within me a flexible heart, so I can serve You in whatever way You lead. Help me become understanding and adaptable, so I may advance Your kingdom wherever I am. Hear my prayer, Father. Through Jesus Christ, our Lord, Amen.*

A Heavenly Connection

As the musicians began setting up their speakers, they suddenly realized there was no power source. During their search, one of them shouted, "Abiel! Look! You won't believe this! There's an old electrical box fastened to this tree." Abiel requested a cord, saying, "Let's see if it works." To their astonishment, when they plugged in the electrical cord, power surged; the lights illuminated, and the speakers crackled with sound. Tears of joy trickled down Abiel's cheeks, as he grasped the full magnitude of what God, the "Divine Master of Ceremonies," had done once again, even providing an electrical connection. They would forever consider it a heavenly connection. God had envisioned a grander display of His power and glory than they had ever imagined.

As the singers tuned their instruments, people who had been watching from the windows of their nearby houses began to gather in what became known as the "tree-lined tabernacle." The laughter of excited children and the barking of several stray dogs blended in joyous harmony. Abiel's faith soared as one by one people arrived. He grabbed a microphone and confidently announced, *"Bienvenidos..."* (Welcome) as strangers found their seats, drawn there by the Spirit. Some began clapping their hands in tune with the music. What a beautiful cathedral it was, with the evening sky as a canopy and a carpet of fragrant, freshly mown grass beneath their feet!

When faced with a great need, it's often in the moments of uncertainty that we witness the most profound examples of divine provision. God has a way of meeting our needs in ways that surpass our understanding and expectations. If He can provide a power source in a place unfamiliar to us, surely He is capable of supplying whatever we require to fulfill the vision He has laid upon our hearts. It's important to have faith and trust in this divine timing and wisdom.

Reflecting on past blessings can be an encouraging exercise. Take a moment to recall a time when a solution or opportunity appeared seemingly out of nowhere—an unexpected blessing that shifted your path in a meaningful way. Remember how that experience felt, the relief, and gratitude it brought.

Take a moment to give thanks, recognizing the blessing as proof of faith's power and God's support. Share this memory with someone you meet today. These stories of unexpected miracles can uplift others and remind us that we are never alone; there is always hope, and with faith, anything is possible.

> **Prayer Response:** *Lord, I know that You are capable of all things, including those beyond our wildest imaginations. While we cannot foresee the future, You can. You lead the way and prepare our paths. Although You may not always answer our prayers according to our specific desires and timing, You hear each one and respond according to Your divine will. I praise You for Your greater plans, which go beyond what we ask or imagine. For now, Lord, I rest assured as a child of God that if You lead me to it in life, You will provide the grace to go through it. In Jesus' name I pray. Amen.*

Thunderstruck Faith

Soon, every chair was occupied, and people were forced to stand as the square overflowed, just as Abiel had envisioned weeks before. Spirited music drifted down the streets and alleys, drawing Latinos of all ages like a modern pied piper. The Kingdom had come to this tiny, Spirit-anointed geo-point.

When the music and singing ended, the crowd listened attentively as Abiel preached a simple Gospel message, proclaiming God's love. He then invited everyone to return next week and bring their families and friends. Just as the musicians began to play again, a flash of lightning ripped through the sky, scattering the crowd. Almost immediately, the heavens opened, and a soaking downpour drenched everyone and their instruments. Within minutes, the fine woods of the guitars had swollen. Surely the guitars were ruined!

As the people dispersed, Abiel was deeply concerned. His friends' guitars were precious and irreplaceable; most of them had saved money for years to purchase those instruments. Abiel was heartsick. They had no choice but to pack the guitars back into their cases as best they could and load them onto the bus with all the other soaking wet equipment. Abiel found himself caught between a moment of misfortune and the desperate need for a miracle. In such times, there are more questions than we care to admit, and the answers can be hard to come by.

C.S. Lewis once remarked, "Miracles are a retelling in small letters of the very same story which is written across the whole world in letters too large for some of us to see." Abiel, experiencing the weight of dampened expectations, chose not to succumb to despair. Instead, he took a moment to pause and seek divine help. When we decide to do this, our minds are rejuvenated, our burdens feel lighter, and we rediscover hope to guide us until we successfully navigate through our challenges. Consider what unexpected storm has erupted in your life today that might be setting the stage for a miracle. Share your struggles with Jesus and open your heart to be amazed by the outcome.

Prayer Response: *God of wind and water, stillness and storm, your Spirit sweeps over the surface of the sea. Grant us the faith to seek you in times of trouble. Extend your hand to us when we are sinking, so that we may believe and worship you. God of compassion, you observe our paths and craft wonders of goodness and grace from even the most terrible events. Through Jesus Christ, Sovereign and Savior. Amen.*[29]

From Calamity to Calm

I cherish the good things in life and praise God for them, but I can't help but question Him when calamity strikes. Why me? Why us? Why this? Why now? It was a dark, stormy night in Tyler, Texas, when a subdued and soggy crew boarded a rain-drenched bus. They were grateful for the crowd and the miraculous provision of power, but everyone was

---

[29] Gleaned from pcusa.org, "Prayers in Times of Trouble or Disaster."

preoccupied with the damage to their waterlogged guitars. Hundreds of dollars were at stake. In such times, remember: Jesus is just as eager to set things right as we are.

The crew finally returned to Dallas in the quiet, early hours after midnight, weary yet grateful. Together, they gathered to thank God for His many blessings, though their prayers were now colored with a fervent plea for resolution to their guitar disaster. With a heavy heart, Abiel tried to find solace in sleep, yet he tossed and turned throughout the night, his prayers for another miracle punctuating the silence sporadically.

As the first rays of dawn began to pierce the sky, his phone rang, jolting him from the restless limbo between waking and slumber. With trepidation, Abiel braced for what he feared would be bad news from one of his guitar-playing friends. Instead, he was taken aback with surprise when his friend's voice, filled with awe, exclaimed, "Abiel, you won't believe this! When I opened my case this morning to inspect my guitar, it was perfectly fine! *God healed my guitar!*"

A wave of relief washed over Abiel as further calls to his other friends brought similar news; their guitars, expected to be damaged from the torrential rain, were unharmed and appeared as if they had never been exposed to the elements. It was a moment that defied explanation but spoke volumes about faith and the boundless possibilities of unseen miracles, restoring not only their instruments but also their spirits.

Thunderstorms of worry can drench our joy when they leave destruction in their wake, but God excels at turning ruin into rejoicing. We can't always choose the trials we face, but by persevering through them, we might find ourselves saying, *"I wouldn't have missed any of them for the world!"* Like Abiel, ask the Lord to forgive you for doubting when circumstances seem bleak. If God can lead to a hidden power source and heal costly guitars, surely He will provide everything you need to accomplish what He is asking of you.

Prayer Response: *Heavenly Father, when my heart is troubled, I will strive to keep it focused on You. In life's unexpected storms, I am grateful that I can always turn to You and find peace and rest. During turbulent times, trials, temptations, weakness, or fear, You are my strength, and Your hiding place is secure. I bless You, Lord, for being my refuge. You are my Strong Tower, Deliverer, and Shelter. I run to You now. Please renew my strength. Guide me with Your Holy Spirit and lead me through my day.*[30] Amen.

Turn Your Setbacks Into Steppingstones

A dedicated group of believers began worshiping in a rented facility. The church was formally established, and Abiel's father became the founding pastor. Meanwhile, we started searching for a permanent site for the church, praying and seeking the right location in the heart of the growing Hispanic community. God guided us to a property that occupied most of a small city block off Bow St. in Tyler, TX. There, we found an abandoned church-like building in ruins, with broken windows and sagging floors. Upon entering for the first time, I was disheartened by the sight of trash, used needles, feces, and the acrid smell of urine. It seemed that only a miracle could restore this building to its original purpose as a house of prayer.

After examining the 1950s wood-frame structure, we concluded that it was beyond saving. However, a setback does not necessarily mean a step back. God may have something better in store for us than we could ever ask for or imagine (Ephesians 3:20).

When you step out to pursue the dream God has given you, be prepared for setbacks and satanic interference. The question remains whether the evil one wages war in a way that delays or otherwise hinders the fulfillment of our prayers.[31] Thomas Watson cautioned, "It

---
30 Adapted from Christianity.com, "25 Prayers for Strength in the Hard and Difficult Times," June 29, 2023.
31 Paul J. Bucknell, "The Hindrances of Satan in Prayer (Daniel 10:13)," Biblical Foundations for Freedom, August 7, 2020.

must not be expected that the devil will let those rest who are laboring to destroy his kingdom." Setbacks are inevitable. C.H. Mackintosh wisely observed, "Wherever God's Spirit is at work, there Satan is sure to be busy. We must remember and ever be prepared for this." It's a reminder that challenges and trials are not partial to anyone—they can touch even the most devout Christians. Even Steve Jobs, a figure not typically associated with religious faith, recognized this universal truth when he said, "Sometimes, life is going to hit you in the head with a brick. Don't lose faith."

When your dreams encounter their first setback, how will you choose to respond? It is tempting to retreat or succumb to discouragement, but instead, let this be a call to persist in prayer. The evil one is adept at employing a myriad of tactics to frustrate, confuse, and hinder us from reaching our potential and fulfilling our purpose. In these moments of struggle, pray earnestly for the grace and resilience to continue moving forward, taking each step with faith and determination.

Keep in mind that setbacks can act as setups for comebacks if we let them refine us instead of define us. Embrace the journey with a heart strengthened by prayer and trust, understanding that perseverance will guide you through challenges and that God's purpose will ultimately prevail. As Mark Batterson said, "When you experience a setback, you may take a step back, but God is already preparing your comeback."

Prayer Response: *Father, in the powerful name of Jesus, I turn to You as I confront the latest setback caused by Satan in my life. I come before You with a heavy heart, burdened by the obstacles and disruptions Satan has placed in my path. Despite his attempts to hinder my progress, I know that he cannot dictate the outcome. With unwavering faith, I seek Your guidance and support, fully believing in Your power and not doubting Your plans. Lift our spirits, O God, and restore our hope, helping us to see this setback for what it truly is—temporary. Grant us the confidence to trust in You wholeheartedly and to cling to the hope we have in Christ Jesus. Amen.*[32] Amen.

---

[32] Adapted from "A Prayer to Pray During a Setback..." Your Daily Prayer, Crosswalk.com, April 21, 2023.

Divine Provision

We felt confident that God had guided us to the right place. The Bow Street property had two additional houses that could be refurbished—one for a parsonage and the other for rental income. The agreed-upon price was fifty thousand dollars. Thankfully, we had some money set aside, but we were still $20,000 short of the amount needed to pay in cash at closing.

Later that week, while I was sitting in my office, puzzled about how to secure the necessary funds, the phone rang. It was Dr. Tom Nees, our Missional Director, who had heard about our mission for the Hispanic community in Tyler. With a touch of sadness, I explained that we were short on cash to finalize the purchase. Without hesitation, Tom asked, *"Would $20,000 help?"*

"Help?!" I exclaimed, immediately apologizing for my outburst. *"That's exactly the amount we need!"* I leaped to my feet, praising the Lord and thanking Tom profusely. Remarkable things happen when we pray and trust God for financial support. "The issue isn't whether God has the money and can help us. It's about what He wants to accomplish in and through us as we depend on Him for what we need. God can take whatever financial situation you're in and build within you character, hope, and a future."[33]

As the story of God's miraculous provision for the Tyler Hispanic project spread, it sparked a wave of inspiration among mission-minded individuals eager to contribute. Generosity, as they discovered, often begets more generosity; it's a contagious spirit that can easily spread from one person to another. Dr. Nees' own generosity served as a catalyst, motivating others to open their hearts and hands in giving.

Considering this, remember to ask largely of God and place your trust in His boundless provision. Let your life be a testimony to the many ways He is Jehovah Jireh—the Lord who provides. Rick Thomas

---

[33] Cindi McMenamin, Crosswalk.com, "8 Ways to Trust God When Money Is Tight," May 31, 2019.

wisely noted, "Right beyond your ability is where God wants you." This is a reminder that God's plan for you doesn't culminate in failure. You haven't come this far to falter.

Pray earnestly and ask wholeheartedly of God. Seek His guidance to discern what He desires for you to do and trust wholeheartedly that He will provide the necessary resources and finances. Embrace the journey with faith, knowing that His provision will meet you at every crossroads and that He will equip you for the paths He has laid out before you.

Prayer Response: *Eternal God, Your word tells me not to worry about what I shall eat, drink, or wear. Therefore, I understand that I should not be anxious about my finances. While others chase after these things, You, my Heavenly Father, know my needs. Lord, You are aware that I require a financial miracle at this moment. I need an abundance of resources—let the drought in my bank account come to an end.*[34] *Amen.*

Vanquishing the Shadows

On a sunny Saturday in Texas, Abiel and I joined an incredible group of men and women from our Richardson church, alongside willing volunteers from Tyler First Nazarene, to complete the takedown of a crack house. I was part of the team responsible for making a final sweep of the floors before the floorboards were removed. It seemed there was even more trash and drug paraphernalia than we had encountered during our previous visit. Many of us had forgotten to bring gloves, so we exercised extreme caution. However, our greatest protection came from the prayer covering we maintained. Miraculously, no one injured themselves with a dirty needle, and no one contracted HIV.

By mid-afternoon, we had achieved our goal of disassembling the house board-by-board. We stacked the salvageable lumber, hoping it

---

[34] Adapted from ConnectUS.com, "25 Powerful Miracle Prayers for Financial Help from God," October 11, 2020.

might be used in building the new church. The house, once a place where drug dealers and users operated undisturbed in the darkness, was lit only by the candles used for boiling crack. Although the building had been physically disassembled, it was only later that we realized the unseen, ruling spirits had not traveled far and had entrenched themselves elsewhere on the property.

In spiritual warfare, we engage with a formidable adversary—an unseen and powerful foe who is much more than the fictional villain portrayed in films. The Bible presents this adversary as a real, malignant angel in defiance of God and His people, conducting his battles on an invisible battleground. Gregory Koukl warns, "The devil gains ground by craftiness and secrecy, and he destroys by lies, accusation, enticement, and subterfuge. If you doubt him, beware. Stealth is his weapon. Satan happily stays in the shadows where he can do his dark business undetected." [35]

It is crucial that we do not remain spiritually blind to this reality. Instead, we must equip ourselves with spiritual discernment and strength to withstand his ploys. The key to standing firm in this unseen battle is to counter lies with truth. By grounding ourselves in the truth of God's Word, we illuminate the shadows where deceit thrives and strip the enemy of his power. Regular prayer, study of the scriptures, and relying on the Holy Spirit for guidance and insight are essential strategies in this spiritual combat. Recognizing the enemy's methods and vulnerabilities allows us to fortify our defenses and remain steadfast in our faith. By embracing truth and rejecting deceit, we become better equipped to resist the enemy's tactics, shielding ourselves with the armor of God's promises and truths.

> **Prayer Response:** *Lord God, I seek to be strengthened in You and in the power of Your might. Thank You for equipping us with spiritual armor to withstand Satan's fiery darts. I am aware that as I pray for Your church, I can expect attacks from the enemy. Please guard and pro-*

---

35 Gregory Koukl, The Story of Reality (Grand Rapids, Zondervan: 2017), 85.

tect me. Help me to remain alert and vigilant, standing firm in the faith. I am grateful for the power of the Holy Spirit, which aids me in resisting the enemy. Thank You for providing Your Word to empower me in this resistance (James 4:7). I submit myself to You, Lord God. I resist the devil, and he will flee from me because You command him to depart. Thank You for the victory through Christ my Lord. Amen.[36]

The Unseen Battle

J.C. Philpot once remarked, "Satan is exceedingly cunning, and his agents surround us in such a way that their schemes are cleverly disguised. Their language is persuasive, their demeanor is beguiling, their appearance often commanding, and their arguments are incredibly subtle. Their relentless activity and keen insight into our weaknesses are matched only by their unwavering hostility towards Christ and His gospel. Their complete absence of principle and honesty means that the net may be closing around us long before we have any suspicion of these diabolical plots against us."[37]

At that time, we were unaware that we had entered a place deeply entrenched by the devil and his forces—a place under Satan's curse. In my naivety about such malevolent environments, I would soon discover that unexplained sickness and infirmity often accompany these strongholds of Satan. Other manifestations include mental confusion, sleeplessness, and recurrent sexually explicit dreams. Workers may experience extreme fatigue and inexplicable negative attitudes. We greatly underestimated the extent of the spiritual warfare arrayed against us.

The god of this age opposes us (Eph. 6:12). Satan's strategy is to thwart our efforts and blind the eyes of those we aim to reach with the Gospel, preventing God from being glorified and keeping the lost from being saved. Our spiritual battles and warfare are indeed real,

---

36 Adapted from Acts 29 Booklet, "Prayer for Resist the Enemy," Asbury Church.
37 J.C. Philpot, A Puritan Golden Treasury, compiled by I.D.E. Thomas, by permission of Banner of Truth, Carlisle, PA. 2000, p. 75.

even though we cannot physically see our attackers. On the invisible battlefield, a war rages regardless of our perceptions. We are either victors or victims. Jesus has already come and conquered; the war is won in the heavens.

We must be vigilant and not fall into ignorance regarding Satan's schemes, as doing so can leave us vulnerable to defeat. Instead, we should seek God's guidance and strength to recognize, confront, and overcome these spiritual challenges. Scripture admonishes us to stay aware and alert: *"Be sober-minded; be watchful"* (1 Pet. 5:8). We are encouraged to put on the full armor of God each day, ensuring that we don't leave home without it.

Commit to this practice today by faith. Take up the Word of God, the sword of the Spirit, as your offensive weapon (Eph. 6:11). This sword equips you to face and combat the deceit and attacks of the enemy with the truth and power of God's Word. Remember, as Lester Sumrall advised, to "resolve never to confess defeat" (2 Cor. 2:14). By embodying this resolve, you embrace the victory that God promises through Christ, reinforcing your spiritual defenses and standing firm against all adversities.

Prayer Response: *Lord, I come before You today, declaring that You redeemed us from the curse of the law by becoming a curse for us, as stated in Galatians 3:13. In Your name, I now claim the full power of Your cross, death, blood, and sacrifice, as well as Your resurrection, life, and empty tomb. I call upon Your authority, rule, and dominion. May You dismantle every wicked power and domain. Let whatever was meant for evil be turned to good through Your mighty name. Amen.*

Confronting the Darkness

Have you ever wondered why it's so challenging to make progress for God? Gregory Brown explains, "Satan employs numerous methods and schemes to attack people. By understanding these tactics, we can become more effective in overcoming them."[38] This spiritual reconnaissance is essential when entering an unseen battlefield. We found ourselves in an unknown drug haven, a place where Satan believed he had a stronghold to exalt himself and ensnare lost souls. By stepping into Satan's territory, we challenged his entrenched forces. A "power encounter" was unfolding in the spiritual realm, and its effects soon became evident. If malevolent spirits inhabit other dark dens of iniquity, they certainly take up residence in crack houses. But where do they go when we dismantle their shelters?

There were two other buildings on the property: a small one-bedroom flat that we refurbished and rented to generate income for the fledgling church, and a larger house that we remodeled into a parsonage for the pastor and his family.

At the time, we thought nothing of it, but strange occurrences began happening in the old parsonage. Church leaders and workers who stayed there fell ill with each visit. Coincidence? Hardly! And was it mere coincidence that Abiel's father, Martin Hernandez, died suddenly in a car accident? Don't be deceived; Satan opposes any good we strive to achieve in Jesus' name. Demons are supernatural (though not all-powerful), wicked (ruthless in pursuing their malicious designs), organized (focused on turning people away from God), and as we discovered, territorial (preferring certain regions, individuals, and possibly even families and cultures).

Facing temptations and spiritual trials is a reality for believers, often coming like a devastating storm as Satan seeks to dispirit us. In these moments, find your strength in God by relying on His promises and presence. Through prayer and Scripture, seek His guidance and protection, and remind yourself of His faithfulness and the victory you have in Him. By anchoring yourself in God's truth and love, you can resist discouragement and maintain your faith. Trust in God as your refuge and strength, and let His support empower you to weather any storm.

---

[38] Gregory Brown, "5. Satan's Methods," Bible.org, January 21, 2023

Prayer Response: *Lord, today I wholeheartedly submit myself to You, declaring my resistance to any satanic attempts to hinder me from doing Your will. You, Your Word, and prayer are my secret weapons, Lord. I belong to You, and this instills in me a powerful confidence in God. I desire to constantly don the spiritual armor You provide. Help me to use it not only to defend myself but also to protect others from Satan's fiery darts. No one and nothing can snatch me away from Your hand. You are my Shield of faith, my ever-present help in times of trouble. Jesus, I receive You anew this day as my Shield. Amen.*[39]

Overcoming Darkness

After Martin's untimely death, we found a pastor in Guatemala and began the lengthy legal process to obtain an R1 Visa for Arnoldo Toj, his wife Edu, and their children. Intercessory prayer again expedited this process. In a remarkably short time, we welcomed the Toj family to Tyler and helped them move their belongings into the newly renovated parsonage. Within a week, however, Edu became gravely ill. At night, strange noises and demonic voices filled the house, robbing them of sleep and tormenting Arnoldo with lurid nightmares. Fear almost paralyzed them. Who can fully grasp the extent to which Satan and his malevolent forces will go?

Yet nearly a thousand prayer partners interceded fervently, joining forces with the Host of Heaven's armies and an interceding Savior at the right hand of the Father, unaware of the battle raging on Bow Street. In his total helplessness and desperation, Arnoldo gathered his family into the living room and prayed in the name of Jesus, commanding any evil spirits or demons that had taken residence in the house to flee.

It is generally unwise to confront an unseen enemy, but when you have no other choice, stand in the Lord's power and witness what happens. Don Stewart advises believers to be vigilant against Satan's at-

---

[39] Adapted from Rebecca Barlow Jordan, "Spiritual Warfare Prayers for Supernatural Help in the Battle."

tacks and to resist when he approaches. "Resist has the idea of withstanding or standing our ground. By standing our ground, Satan can be overcome."[40] Confess your dependency on God and God alone. Stand tall in His power. Demonic power at its strongest is weak, while the Christian's true power, even at its weakest, is strong. You have already won because the Lord has already won. Rest confidently in the knowledge that Jesus will fight the battle for you, your church, and your family.

> **Prayer Response:** *Dear Heavenly Father, I seek Your divine protection from the wickedness of the evil one. You are Almighty God, and his power is insignificant compared to the might You wield. I come to Your refuge with joy, for You shelter me against the attacks of the devil. Protect me, O Lord, from the cunning schemes of the enemy, and save me from his evil plots. Envelop me in Your presence when I feel weak, so that he will flee from my vicinity. Keep us beyond the reach of his harmful intentions and cradle us in the safety of Your loving hands. Amen.*[41]

Unconquerable with Christ

No plan formed against us can succeed! If God is for us, who or what can stand against us? Absolutely nothing can stop us. The Apostle Paul declared that we are "super conquerors" through Christ who loves us (Romans 8:37). Think of the most terrifying thing that this world or any other world can produce. Not one of these things can separate us from God's love!

In the Bow Street parsonage, Arnoldo, huddled with his family in a circle of prayer, cried out to God in the name of Jesus for protection and deliverance. In that moment of powerful prayer, he and his family, as well as the house they called home, were set free. By the authority of Christ's victory on the cross, Pastor Toj commanded any enemies of Christ that had been sent or assigned to that house to leave. They strapped on the full armor of God, claimed Christ's victory on the

---

40 Don Stewart, "How Can the Believer Have Victory over the Devil?" Blue Letter Bible.
41 Adapted from Crosswalk.com, "25 Prayers for Protection Against Evil," February 10, 2020.

cross, and proceeded to reclaim Bow Street as the Kingdom of Christ territory.

John MacArthur underscores the crucial need to understand our enemy, likening it to how every military leader carefully examines intelligence on the adversary prior to engaging in battle.[42] The Bible serves as our comprehensive intelligence report on Satan, meaning that ignorance will never serve as an acceptable excuse for defeat. God provides Christians with a substantial advantage through detailed information about the enemy. Arnoldo was well-aware of both Satan's capabilities and limitations, as well as the diverse methods he employs.

Desecration can be uprooted, and evil spirits, which pollute places with their unholy presence, can indeed be driven out. Your home has the potential to transform into an oasis filled with the Lord's Presence, serving as a sanctuary that offers protection from demonic interference. It is crucial to understand that any servant of Jesus who significantly threatens the forces of hell will inevitably become a target, encountering resistance, particularly during crucial moments in their ministry. Despite this, when light and darkness engage in conflict, it is always Jesus, the Light, who prevails and emerges victorious!

Prayer Response: *Almighty God, please help me never forget Who you are. I take my position and stand firm. I know You are fighting this battle for me. Thank you for placing all the gifts and powers of heaven at my disposal. When we face enemies in the form of obstacles and challenges that seem greater than we are, we will not be afraid. You Lord are with us! We will not lose heart, panic, or tremble, for we know You will fight for us against our enemies, and You will give us victory! With Your help we will do mighty things; we will trample down our foes, in Jesus' mighty name. Amen*[43]

---

42 MacArthur, J., & Mayhue, R. (Eds.). (2017). Biblical Doctrine: A Systematic Summary of Bible Truth (pp. 685–686). Wheaton, IL: Crossway.
43 Kingdombuilders.com, "A Declaration of Victory," Windsor Village Church, August 1, 2022.

Conquering Crack Hill

There are no assurances that your efforts for God will be effortless. The notion that God often calls us to challenging and risky tasks challenges the misconception that spiritual paths are always safe and comfortable. True faith may require courage to undertake difficult missions in daunting places. Anticipate challenges and hardships. The Evil One aims to disorient, distract, and discourage us, with the ultimate goal of derailing or destroying us.

The night before the windows were to be installed in the new metal building, they were delivered without anyone present to receive them. As darkness fell, thieves took advantage of the situation and stole the windows. When a police officer arrived to take the report, he shook his head in dismay and said,

"You do know you invaded Crack Hill, don't you?"

It was then that we fully grasped the magnitude of our challenge. Despite Satan's relentless opposition, Christ our King emerged victorious over Crack Hill!

We are aware of satan's schemes, as Paul reminds us in 2 Corinthians 2:11. Expecting no resistance when pursuing God-sized goals is foolish. Challenges are an inevitable part of this journey. However, with steadfast faith and perseverance, victory through Christ is assured. We chose not to take the path of least resistance, even though it demanded an arduous uphill climb. Step by step, we relied on God's strength and power to guide us.

Any servant of Jesus who poses a threat to the powers of hell is bound to become a target, encountering resistance, especially during strategic moments of their ministry. However, when light and darkness collide, it is always Jesus, the Light, who prevails! Day in and day out, the enemy continued his assaults, but we had learned to pray and persevere, moving forward with Jesus as our guide. Occasionally, Satan launches a full-scale attack, as he did against the Toj family during their very first week. If he cannot defeat you one way, he will undoubtedly try another. Despite these challenges, Arnoldo and Edu Toj continue to faithfully serve at Vida a Las Naciones (Life to the Nations) to this very day!

> **Prayer Response:** *Lord, I thank You for being the source of my help. As the Maker of heaven and earth, You are also the architect of my family. Please guide us to honor and glorify You in all that we do. Help us to live lives that are pleasing to You each day. Jesus, we acknowledge that without You, we can do nothing. All our help and strength come from You, the Creator of heaven and earth (Ps. 121). Nothing takes You by surprise or escapes Your watchful eye. You are aware of everything, including the devil's schemes to steal, kill, and destroy Your people (1 Pet. 5:8; John 10:10). Not us, not now—neither me nor my church. In Your powerful name, Amen.*[44]

---

[44] Adapted from Garmentsofsplendor.com, "How to Pray Psalm 121 for Your Family," September 25, 2020.

3

How to Operate at Full Capacity

C.H. Spurgeon once observed with lament that the full capacity of prayer power remains untested. If we desire to witness grand displays of divine power and grace within realms of weakness, failure, and disappointment, let us rise to answer God's enduring challenge: *"Call to Me, and I will answer you and tell you great and unsearchable things you do not know." (Jer. 33:3, NLT)*

There is no doubt that it is time for us to renew our faith in God's immense power, rather than first attempting to solve our own problems or those of our loved ones on our own. We must focus on deepening our intercession and let the Holy Spirit accomplish what only He can, thereby unleashing the supernatural in our circumstances.

This journey is about letting God be God—not that He needs our permission. The more quickly we acknowledge that not every issue has a human solution, the better off we will be. God's way is always the best way. Sometimes, what He requires from us is not our attempt at assistance, but for us to step aside, call on Him, and trust that He will answer and reveal to us great and mighty things we do not yet know.

Prayer Response: *God Almighty, my heart is overwhelmed with worries and uncertainties due to the situation I find myself in. I feel confused, alone, restless, and hopeless as I sink deeper into the problems I am currently facing. Each attempt I make to solve these issues seems futile as they neither diminish nor improve. I have made plans on my own, but all of them have failed. I realize now, my Lord, that it is because I did not include You in my planning.[1] In Jesus' name. Amen.*

Pray in Agreement

The concept of agreement praying finds its roots in the Bible, specifically in Matthew 18:19-20, where Jesus states, *"If two of you agree on earth concerning anything you ask, it will be done for you by My Father in heaven. For where two or three are gathered in my name, there I am with them."*

Once you discover the power of praying in agreement and begin to witness miraculous results, you will never be content to settle for anything less. It only takes two people, though more is even better. "The key to power in praying together is a unified focus," affirms Debbie Przybylski. "Prayerful agreement leads to breakthroughs." She uses the analogy of an orchestra tuning up to illustrate this point. Having played in a band, I am familiar with the chaos and noise that occurs when every instrument plays its own part independently. However, when the conductor raises the baton, the instruments immediately harmonize.[2] This is how prayer should be when Jesus is the conductor of our gatherings. Today could be the day you discover how to harness God's powerful formula for breakthrough in prayer. Let us explore and embrace the secret of agreement!

The Kendrick brothers highlight the incredible potential of prayer, asserting that "Prayer means that God's miracle-working power is always a possible solution to whatever challenge stands before us." They

---
1 Adapted from AvePray, "Prayer for help with problems I'm currently facing," September 15, 2022.
2 Debbie Przybylski, "Prayer Agreement Leads to Breakthrough," Crosswalk.com, April 18, 2017.

further emphasize that "Prayer infuses all our efforts and the genuine concerns of our hearts with God's boundless ability." For them, prayer represents hope, help, relief, and power—immense power at that. This perspective encourages us to rely on prayer as a vital and dynamic force in our lives, capable of transforming situations and aligning us with God's will and strength.[3]

Discovering the transformative power of prayer is perhaps the greatest revelation you can experience in your Christian journey. This divine inheritance is accessible to any believer who heeds the call of Hebrews 4:16. This scripture invites us to boldly approach God's throne of grace with confidence, affirming that we truly belong there. While maintaining a private prayer life is essential, we must also recognize the unique strength found in public prayer. Oliver W. Price emphasized that "Private prayer is necessary. But we also need to pray with others, striving to unite under the headship of Christ and His shepherd care."[4] Gathering in prayer with others allows us to listen to one another in God's presence, creating a profound and shared spiritual experience. This unity under Christ underscores the importance of communal prayer and the deep connections it fosters among believers.

The challenge of coming together in united prayer efforts is often attributed to spiritual opposition, as Satan understands the immense power that comes from prayer agreement. Agreement signifies unity, which can unleash exponential and synergistic power. As Chidi Okoroafor points out, "Exponential and synergistic power is unleashed through the Prayer of Agreement."[5] This highlights the importance of believers coming together with a shared purpose in prayer, as it amplifies their spiritual impact and draws upon the collective strength of their faith. This understanding encourages Christians to overcome any hindrances to unity and fully embrace the powerful potential of praying together in agreement.

Prayer Response: *Father, I trust in the power of*

---
[3] Stephen and Alex Kendrick, The Battle Plan for Prayer, 18-19.
[4] Op. Cit., Price, 19.
[5] Chidi Okoroafor, "Prayer of agreement," The Guardian, August 11, 2019.

agreement in prayer as Your Word teaches. Please guide me to a friend who will join me in seeking Your guidance. Help us to pray obediently according to Your direction. We long to hear from You and to be led by the Holy Spirit in our prayers. In Jesus' name, Amen.

Revitalizing Worship

Though the Book of Acts is a record of Spirit-guided action, the first chapter pauses for a prayer meeting. The apostles and followers of Jesus obeyed His command to wait in Jerusalem for the promise of the Father (Acts 1:4-5). United in prayer, they believed that Christ is present whenever two or three gather in His name. Christ attends church and is ready to take charge if we genuinely seek Him in prayer. When we allow the Holy Spirit to take an active role, worship is transformed, and worshippers are transformed into active participants.

Do not treat prayer as ancillary to worship, as if it were irrelevant, or it will inevitably become "the stepchild of corporate worship." Instead, make prayer an integral part of worship, for "by that omission, we declare its value as insignificant." Bishop Small laments, "Regrettably, too little prayer takes place in our corporate worship. Even when we sing prayerful songs, we merely recite the lyrics instead of praying them. Though God is present in the room, we remain unconscious of His presence, essentially ignoring Him. We engage in discussions about Him with one another, yet we fail to converse directly with Him."[6]

On the Day of Pentecost, during a prayer meeting, the Church was established as God intended—a house of prayer for all nations. However, what have we turned it into? Houses of preaching and singing, rather than houses of prayer. Our efforts to put on impressive services seem to yield minimal results in terms of making disciples.

Mike Erre's observation in *Death by Church* suggests that a sig-

---

[6] Excerpts from a blog by P. Douglas Small entitled, "What Does Prayer Look Like in Your Worship Service?" dated 5/19/18.

nificant portion of people attending religious events, including church services, act as passive observers rather than active participants. The COVID-19 pandemic in 2020 further intensified this issue, with more individuals engaging in worship from a distance and potentially slipping into a spectator mindset. This shift underscores the necessity of ending the "self-deception" of treating worship merely as an event to watch. Bishop Small warns against "narcissistic self-interested worship," which he defines as a form of idolatry or "self-worship, thinly disguised."

To counteract this trend, active engagement in prayer is essential. Prayer acts as a transformative key that shifts us from passive spectators to active, fully invested participants in our spiritual lives. By fostering a personal and communal connection through prayer, worship becomes a vibrant, interactive experience, enabling believers to connect more deeply with their faith and community. This transformation highlights the essential role prayer plays in revitalizing worship as an act of genuine engagement rather than mere observation.

Prayer Response: *Lord, today I choose to praise and worship You. You know how to break through the difficulties in my life. I choose not to be overwhelmed by circumstances, but instead, I choose to behold Your beauty and greatness. I will join my fellow worshipers in blessing Your holy name as we worship in spirit and in truth.*[7] *In Jesus' name. Amen.*

Worshiping in Spirit and Truth

In many churches, including my own, worship has evolved into a form of "spectator sport." Without musical notes to guide them—a challenge for those unfamiliar with reading music—many congregants remain passive during new or complex hymns, simply standing or sitting in silence instead of joining in the singing. However, a transformation occurs when the words to a familiar hymn like *"It Is Well with My*

---

[7] Adapted from Debbie Przybylski, "Worship Prayers - Experience Breakthroughs in Praise," Crosswalk.com, June 8, 2018.

Soul" appears on the screens. Suddenly, those previously silent mouths start singing with conviction.

Bishop Small, my foremost mentor in prayer, articulates a crucial warning: "In our efforts to be contemporary and engage a post-Christian culture, we risk mirroring it, potentially diluting our own faith. By centering worship around the individual—a sinner inherently plagued by self-centeredness—we only fuel the very sin we aim to overcome. Instead, what is essential is a profound shift toward repentance, humility, embracing the cross, and the extinguishing of both sin and self-centeredness."[8]

Incorporating "significant prayer moments" into worship services is a vital step towards transforming passive observance into active participation. It involves moving beyond just singing prayerful songs to genuinely engaging with the prayers woven into those songs, fostering a direct and meaningful interaction with God. It's possible to attend church and remain disconnected from God's presence. Therefore, intentionality in building a dialogue with God is essential.

Encouraging personal devotion to prayer and fostering it within the community truly transforms lives. When we pray together, we're drawn closer to worshiping God in spirit and truth, building a collective reliance on Him. This not only deepens our faith but turns us from mere observers into active participants in our spiritual journeys.

The early church, as described in Acts 1:14, set a precedent by making prayer central to its gatherings, not an afterthought. Regular corporate prayer is crucial for nurturing a spiritually vibrant community of faith and fostering deep connections with God and each other. In this way, the practice of incorporating significant prayer moments becomes a catalyst for discipleship, community, and spiritual growth, aligning modern worship practices more closely with the original intent and spirit of the early church.

Prayer Response: *"Teach me to ascend to Your throne*

---
[8] Small, "What Does Prayer Look Like in Your Worship Service?"

room in worship and then descend back into the harvest field here on earth, praying and striving for victory in every aspect of life. Help me cultivate a lifestyle of worship, always giving thanks to You in every situation. I believe that worshipping You is crucial for breakthroughs in all areas of my life. I trust in the power of worship and know that Your truth resides in a heart that worships. I offer You a sacrifice of praise at this moment. Blessed be the name of the Lord. In Jesus' name, Amen."[9]

Opening Heaven's Resources

During one of our prayer meetings, we paused to remind ourselves of the reason we pray: because Jesus himself prayed. To follow in Jesus' footsteps, we too must engage in prayer. Our prayers lead to profound and eternally significant outcomes. Prayer does more than simply amplify our individual efforts; it often serves as the defining factor between defeat and victory. If we aspire to achieve spiritual victories, it is essential that we be brought to our knees.

Our best efforts are not equivalent to anything God can accomplish. Prayer has the power to open doors that might otherwise remain closed. Therefore, it is essential to incorporate prayer into every worship gathering with both variety and consistency. Do not neglect your greatest resource. Never treat Almighty God as a last resort when He delights in being your first resource! God has made supply dependent on prayer. It is the mechanism through which believers access heaven's resources from Christ's inheritance. You are rich, but you act as though you are poor when you neglect to pray.

We may not fully grasp just how much prosperity has diminished the practice of prayer in our lives. Philip Yancey points out, "The wealthy depend on their talent and resources to address immediate challenges, while relying on insurance policies and retirement plans to ensure their future security."[10] This reliance on our own capabilities

---
9 Adapted from Przybylski, "Worship Prayers - Experience Breakthroughs in Praise."
10 Yancey, Prayer, 15.

and safety nets makes me wonder: What miracles might we be missing because we only attempt what our own strength and resources can achieve?

Navigating the major life change of retirement, especially when it involves selling your home and facing financial uncertainties, can indeed be daunting. To fully receive all that He offers, obedience is crucial. If God knows He will receive the glory, He will bless you beyond your abilities and resources. When we step beyond self-reliance and entrust our challenges to Him, we open the door to blessings and miracles that far exceed our limited understanding and capabilities.

Prayer Response: *Heavenly Father, forgive me for the times I didn't turn to You first. You've taught me through my falls and failures. Thank You for Your patience. I'm learning to access heaven's boundless resources, and I'm grateful for Your guidance in prayer. It's as simple as seeking, knocking, and asking in Jesus' name. Amen and Amen.*

Your Anywhere Altar

When my appointment to Southern Florida came through, I had deepened my relationship with the Lord so profoundly that He began revealing events to me before they occurred. Such specific revelations from God are unforgettable. By staying close to Him, you too may be granted insights into future happenings. God eventually led me back to my home state for the final leg of my long journey as a leader of His people.

After a farewell dinner with key leaders, we bid our goodbyes and set off southeast on I-20. Hurricane Katrina had caused significant devastation, prompting us to take a longer route east before heading south. This extended journey provided ample time for solitude, silence, and prayer. Pastor Tommy remarked, "There are altars everywhere we look. In every direction, altars abound, and they become visible whenever we focus our attention on God, centering on gratitude and worship."[11]

The steering wheel of my car became an altar, a sacred space where the Lord could speak when He had my full attention. Amid the silence, the Lord, my source of peace, posed a question:

"Now David," He whispered, *"you waited several years to initiate prayer partners in Dallas… How long will you wait in Southern Florida?"*

Without hesitation, I promised to begin immediately. I had my marching orders. As soon as I started my introductory tour of the churches, I began to enlist prayer partners. Those who believed in the power of prayer readily signed commitment cards at each church I visited, and I carried home a fistful of them each Sunday night. You can build an altar anywhere, and if you travel often, don't be surprised: when you turn off the radio, God may show up, offering clear guidance and direction for the next step in your journey of grace.

The next time you find yourself traveling alone, consider setting aside this journey as an opportunity for spiritual reflection and connection. Begin the trip by spending the first fifteen minutes immersed in Christian music. Let the melodies and lyrics wash over you, creating a peaceful and worshipful atmosphere within your car. This music can help center your thoughts and prepare your heart for a deeper encounter with God.

Once those initial fifteen minutes have passed, gently turn off the music and embrace the silence. Allow the stillness to envelop you as you quiet your mind and spirit before God. Imagine your steering wheel transforming into an altar, a sacred space where you can lay down your thoughts, worries, and praises. In this moment of tranquility, open yourself up to listening for God's voice, being attentive to any nudges or insights He might offer you.

As you listen, be ready to respond with obedience to whatever guidance or inspiration you receive. Whether it's a new perspective on a situation, a calling to act in kindness, or simply a renewed sense of

---

11 Pastor Tommy, "Altars Everywhere," flintasbury.org, Feb 3, 2017.

peace, embrace it wholeheartedly. The purpose of this time is not just to listen but to carry out what you feel led to do, allowing this journey to be more than just a physical trip, but a spiritual voyage as well.

> **Prayer Response:** *Father, I ask that Your Holy Spirit alone speaks to me as I seek Your wisdom, insight, and direction. I am silencing all distractions so that I may hear Your whisper. Please grant me the grace to obey promptly whatever You reveal to me or direct me to do. The most important thing is that I obey Your voice. If I am unsure or need further confirmation, I ask for Your guidance. However, if I clearly receive Your direction, I will respond with full obedience, confident that the Holy Spirit is guiding me. In Jesus' mighty name, Amen.*[12]

The "Magic Carpet" of Prayer

Upon reaching a thousand prayer partners and making my inaugural trip to Africa, I began to ponder the ideal number of intercessors to recruit. The work God was accomplishing on the frontlines of prayer in Southern Florida extended into my teaching sessions on *Walking the Leadership Higher Ground* at Africa Nazarene University in January 2006.[13] Nairobi church pastor Julius Nguki and his congregation of 200 expressed a desire to partner with us and gifted me a colorful belt. *"Whenever you wear it,"* he explained, *"let it remind you that we are praying for you."* Although I had traveled to Kenya with the intention of serving, I ended up receiving far more than I gave. The intercession of my prayer partners provided me with strength, power, and anointing for both teaching and preaching.

Prayer is indeed more than just a priority; it's a vital lifeline that connects us to God and aligns our hearts with His will. When we pray, especially in unity with others, we not only reach out to God but also bring Him joy as our collective voices rise with one heart and mind.

---

[12] Jim Harrison, "Listening Prayer Helps You Hear God More Clearly. Here's How," Faithward.
[13] Walking the Leadership Higher Ground is available on Amazon.com.

The example of the Kenyans feeling a spiritual compulsion to join in prayer for their distant brothers and sisters illustrates the profound impact and reach of intercessory prayer. It transcends geographical boundaries, allowing us to support and uplift others across the globe through what can be described as the "magic carpet" of prayer. Intercessory prayer allows us to support others worldwide. If you haven't experienced the power of intercessors praying for you, consider starting today by inviting at least two people to join you in prayer for your next ministry opportunity. Seek God's guidance on whom to partner with in prayer. Praying with and for others not only strengthens your efforts but also refreshes and encourages all believers involved, fostering a sense of community and shared purpose.

Prayer Response: *Father, I come boldly to Your throne of grace, accepting Your standing invitation (Hebrews 4:16). I am painfully aware of how often I rely solely on my own efforts. I humbly ask for Your forgiveness and pray that You enable me, through Your Holy Spirit, to trust in Your power to accomplish what is beyond my abilities. Guide me to join with other believers in prayer. The possibilities are vast and extend far beyond my natural limitations, especially when I consider that You are always searching for opportunities to show Your strength on my behalf (1 Chronicles 16:9). You have even been known to turn the impossible into the possible. In the meantime, I will live in the power of Christ, in whose name I pray. Amen.*

Prayer Enhances Effectiveness

It is said that Charles Finney frequently dispatched Daniel Nash, known as "the prevailing prince of prayer," to prepare locations and people for Finney's revival campaigns. Often, Nash would spend three to four weeks in prayer to get the area ready. Why? Because intercession opens doors and enhances effectiveness. Frequently, Nash would not attend the meetings but would instead pray for the outpouring of the Spirit upon Finney as he preached. While Finney delivered his sermons, "Nash devoted himself almost continuously to prayer."

Finney is recognized as the father of American revivalism, and his work provided a significant impetus to "American modernization."[14] When a Holy God draws near during genuine revival, individuals undergo a deep and profound conviction of sin, akin to Isaiah's experience in the presence of a holy God (Isaiah 6:1). We need an acute awareness of God's presence and holiness, which leads to spiritual awakening. This underscores the necessity of preparatory prayer. "Let holy preparation link hands with patient expectation," said C. H. Spurgeon, "and we shall have far larger answers to our prayers."

Prayer preparation was a fundamental component of Billy Graham's evangelistic crusades. For many years, Sterling Huston oversaw these crusades across the United States and Canada. In his book *"Crusade Evangelism and the Local Church,"* he emphasizes, "Prayer is the foremost priority in evangelism. People, methods, and materials are merely tools; it is only through prayer that these tools become effective through the empowerment of the Holy Spirit."

Intercessory prayer not only transforms the intercessor but also unleashes God's power into the lives of those we aim to reach with the Gospel. It is essential for claiming the victory provided by Christ. Therefore, include prayer preparation as a crucial part of planning any Kingdom endeavor. Pray for supernatural success in your upcoming ventures and wait patiently to witness what God can accomplish.

> **Prayer Response:** *Lord, I raise the flag of praise high and proclaim that You are my King. I boldly advance into Your kingdom, trusting in You as my fortress. I stand firm, rooted in the goodness of Your love, and draw near to You. I ride triumphantly upon Your grace, grateful that the battle has already been won. You are my King, my fortress, my strength, and my Redeemer. Lord, I exalt Your name above all others and worship You.!*[15] *Amen and Amen.*

---

14 James H. Moorehead, Journal of Presbyterian History (1962-1985) © 1984, 95.
15 Lords-prayer-words.com, "Prayer for Victory and Protection," Prayer for Victory."

More and Better Prayer

A church in Arizona randomly selected 80 families and committed to praying for them over a period of three months. At the end of the 90 days, they assessed the impact of their prayers. They contacted the families to ask permission to send a team to pray for any needs they might have, without pressuring them to accept Christ or attend church. The team's goal was to request prayer requests at the doorstep and offer a brief prayer on the family's behalf.

Additionally, 80 families who had not been prayed for over the 90-day period were also contacted. Among these, only one responded positively. However, among the families who had been the subjects of prayer, 69 invited the prayer team to their home, and of those, 45 welcomed the team inside. Wesley L. Duewel concluded, "Prayer is the only adequate way to multiply our efforts fast enough to reap the harvest God desires."

Prayer opens doors and softens hearts. Without prayer, opportunities and guidance from the Spirit are rare or absent. Years ago, R. A. Torrey asserted, "We live in a day characterized by the multiplication of man's machinery and the diminution of God's power. The great cry of our day is work, work, work! Organize, organize, organize! Give us some new society! Tell us some new methods! Devise some new machinery! But the great need of our day is prayer—more prayer and better prayer."[16] Doors will open when we ask, seek, and knock (Luke 11:9-10), but someone must pay the price of prayer. Keep praying for the lost to prevent Satan from blocking the truth. Understand that prayer is a privilege, not a burden, so do not grow weary praying for the lost and broken.

At a Camp meeting, I asked if anyone had stopped praying for a lost loved one because it seemed impossible. An elderly lady said she had renewed her commitment to pray for her lost grandson. Our

---

[16] Cited in Stewart Robinson, "Praying the Price," Renewal Journal, 27 February 2016.

greatest successes in the Kingdom come not by might or power, but by the gracious release of Holy Spirit power (Zechariah 4:6). If we seek growth, fervent and united prayer is essential.

> **Prayer Response:** *Father God, I thank You for granting me the privilege of being part of this high kingdom priority. Prayer is a royal privilege that yields amazing results. I am willing to stand in the gap as an intercessor. I will enter my prayer closet and devote myself wholeheartedly. Please help me to remain faithful in my prayer life. May my prayers be filled with faith and align with Your will. In Jesus' name, Amen.*

Specific and Strategic Prayer

Effective prayer partners offer the most powerful intercessions when they base their prayers on precise and accurate information. Just like fuel ignites a fire, information energizes prayer. Therefore, when you request someone to pray, it is crucial to clearly articulate what you need them to pray for. This method has led to substantial advancements in the kingdom for many believers. Over a decade ago, I started documenting the answers to my prayers, and I am immensely thankful for this practice. When your prayers are specific, your praise and thanksgiving should be equally detailed when God responds. When praying, we should feel empowered to ask God boldly and specifically for our needs, expressing our desires with fervor and sincerity, while also diligently accepting and trusting in God's wise and loving plan for us. Keeping a record of our prayer requests can deepen our spiritual journey, allowing us to see tangible evidence of the answers we receive and giving us more reasons to celebrate our faith together.

Anna Burgess emphasizes the power and effectiveness of prayer, stating, "Prayer is powerful and effective if we actually engage in it." She advises that "if we genuinely want to witness breakthroughs of the kingdom in our lives and the lives of others, we need to be strategic in our prayers. The kingdom of God advances through both prayer and action—much like two legs on a person; while you can get somewhere by hopping, it isn't very effective!" Therefore, she suggests making your prayer requests specific.[17]

Keeping a journal for prayer requests is an incredibly beneficial practice. Once you begin documenting the responses to your prayers, don't be surprised if your journal evolves into a hymnal of praise. When I am asked to pray for specific matters and commit to doing so, I make it a point to record and date each request. This habit not only reminds me to pray but also prompts me to thank God when He answers.

Herbert Lockyer, in his book *All the Prayers of the Bible*, notes that there are 450 specific answers to 650 prayers recorded in the Bible. By starting to record your requests and the corresponding answers, you will witness firsthand just how faithful God is in listening and responding. If you believe in the power of petition, take another step and discover the power of praise when God answers your prayers.

If you don't already maintain a prayer list, start one. Note the date when you make the request and the date when it is answered. This practice will significantly boost your faith. As C.H. Spurgeon wrote, "Prayer is the breath, the watchword, the comfort, the strength, the honor of a Christian."

Learn to pray with specificity and strategic intent, and you will unleash the power of God.

> **Prayer Response:** *Father, this concept is unfamiliar to me. I have seldom thought about praying with intentionality and specificity. Please guide me to be more deliberate in recording the answers to my prayers. Teach me how to express praise and gratitude to You whenever I seek and receive responses to my prayers. May Your praise always be on my lips, for You hear and answer my prayers. I ask this in Jesus' name. Amen.*

---
17 Anna Burgess website, "4 Steps to Strategically Pray and See."

How to Avoid the Leprosy of Ingratitude

One solitary leper returned to thank Jesus for his miraculous healing, completing the process with his gratitude (Luke 17:17-19). Unlike him, I often found myself resembling the nine ungrateful lepers. I knew I didn't want to be an unthankful person—consistently negative, prone to chronic complaining, never fully appreciating what God has given me, and always craving more.

I didn't start recording answers to my prayers until 2007. However, three years ago, after reading Mark Batterson's excellent book *If,* I converted my prayer journal into a Gratitude Journal. I realized I needed to practice the daily discipline of finding at least one thing to be thankful for. Gratitude changes our perspective when we pray and removes the leprosy of ingratitude. Even if God never answered another prayer I prayed, I already have a book full of the blessings He has bestowed upon me.

Keeping a record of answered prayers helps me maintain an attitude of gratitude. As Batterson advises, "Number each blessing you receive over the course of a year." This practice helps me remember to be thankful. Journal your answers to prayer, but don't forget the blessings you received from God's gracious hand without even asking. Your gratitude or blessing journal should include both the prayers answered and the unexpected blessings.

Henri Nouwen wrote, "Gratitude as a discipline involves a conscious choice." It's a choice you can make too. Don't assume God already knows how grateful you are. Gratitude stabilizes our emotions and has a transformative effect; complaints turn into praises, and attitudes follow. Before you ask God for anything today, find five things you are thankful for. "Enter into His gates with thanksgiving and His courts with praise" (Psalm 100:4, KJV). Consider making this a daily practice. I did, and the benefits have been amazing.

Prayer Response: *Thank you, Lord, for the abundant blessings you have bestowed upon my life. You have provided me with far more than I could ever have imagined. You have surrounded me with people who consistently look out for my well-being. You have blessed me with family and friends who uplift me each day with their kind words and actions. They inspire me to keep my eyes focused on You and elevate my spirit. Additionally, thank You, Lord, for ensuring my safety. You guide me to make better choices and have placed wise advisors in my life to help me navigate difficult decisions. You communicate with me in countless ways, making me always aware of Your presence. I am profoundly grateful for all the blessings You have granted me. I pray that You continue to remind me of my blessings and never allow me to forget to express my gratitude through prayer and acts of kindness.[18] In Jesus' name. Amen.*

Make Gratitude Your Default Setting

Paul characterizes human sin as a failure to give thanks, highlighting its significance through the concept of "cosmic ingratitude" (Rom.1:21). This, of course, refers to the false belief that one is spiritually self-sufficient. Those who engage in prayer tap into their greatest resource, "wisdom from above" (Jas. 3:17), as opposed to foolishness and confusion. Gratitude is a choice we consciously make, one that can profoundly transform our lives.

The rewards of gratitude surpass the effort it demands. By embracing daily gratitude, we enhance our lives and interactions, gaining a positive outlook. Regular prayer deepens our gratitude and attunement to answered prayers, while mindless ingratitude leads to a diminished life. Gratitude is our key to combating spiritual poverty. Verbal and conscious expressions of thanksgiving for God's grace have a transformative effect on us. Your life will change if you make gratitude your default setting.

---

18 Adapted from Kelli Mahoney, "Show My Gratitude," Jesuitresource.org, Gratitude Prayers.

Over a decade ago, I chose to actively focus on gratitude, leading to a Gratitude Journal with over 700 pages and nearly 700,000 words. Gratitude grows with time and consistent practice, often referred to as "a discipline that changes disposition." This practice fosters a mindset deeply aware of God's grace.

Gary Allen Henecke once cautioned, "Never leave the presence of God in frustration." Instead, leave His presence knowing that God has heard and will answer. The hope we have is not a maybe. God-directed, humbly expressed gratitude is a form of praise. Gratitude, often seen as "the rarest of all virtues," offers overwhelmingly positive benefits. It's easier to complain than to seek out reasons for gratitude, especially during challenging times. We should frequently express our thanks to God and others. Consider conducting a gratitude experiment for ten days to observe changes in your attitude. To operate at full capacity, begin and end your prayers today with praise, "the Alpha and Omega of prayer."

> **Prayer Response:** *Holy Spirit, open my heart to understand how precious and loved I am by You. Illuminate the eyes of my soul to recognize the gifts You have placed before me today. Grant me the grace to perceive each encounter with You and to respond with a grateful heart. Teach me to cultivate gratitude and to embody generosity, mirroring Your boundless generosity towards me. Guide me to collaborate with You in serving my sisters and brothers, all for Your greater glory.[19] In the matchless name of Jesus, Amen.*

The Power and Purpose of Prayer

Let us never forget the significance and intent of prayer if we aim to grow in faith and increase our answered prayers. Daily, continuous prayer should become part of our rhythm and routine. Therefore, let us resolve to take the following steps:

---

[19] Adapted from Rebecca Ruiz, "Teach Me Gratitude," Jesuitresource.org, Gratitude Prayers.

1. Discover the profound richness and significance of prayer.

In discovering the greatness and richness of prayer, we recognize it as a profound acknowledgment of God's immeasurable greatness. As Keller puts it, "Since God is omnipresent and infinitely great, prayer must permeate all aspects of our lives." This practice builds our confidence that God is carefully shaping our lives, turning our hardships into blessings, securing our blessings, and promising that the best is yet to come.[20]

2. Delight in making prayer a daily practice.

Let us be inspired by Jesus to make prayer a daily discipline, as He too was dedicated to prayer. Emulating Jesus in this way means regularly engaging in heartfelt communication with God, who is love. According to E. Stanley Jones, prayer aligns us with God's purpose and power, transforming our perspectives and our actions. It deepens our commitment as we allow God to work within us and through us in ways we could never manage alone. By embracing this spiritual discipline, we gradually evolve and grow. I think William James was right when he said, "The reason why we pray is simply that we cannot help praying." Together, let's cherish and practice daily prayer, delighting in our profound connection with God, who is the essence of love itself.

3. Devote yourself to prayer, trusting that nothing of eternal significance happens without it.

Prayer is essential for Christians, elevating our capabilities and transforming our efforts into victories. Regular, persistent prayer is key, as occasional prayer often fails to tap into its full potential. Without prayer, we're just relying on our own limited strength.

Prayer opens doors that might otherwise remain closed, particularly in areas where we aim for outreach and ministry. Let's reflect on whether we maintain a regular, faithful, and fervent prayer life. If not, we should consider why that might be the case. Let's confess to God that we need His help to cultivate a more consistent prayer practice.

---
20 Timothy Keller, Prayer, 28, 73.

We should acknowledge the areas in our lives where we need guidance and support and ask for His presence to strengthen our commitment to prayer.

> **Prayer Response:** *Father, I believe that You have endowed me with power, love, and self-control. I desire to utilize these remarkable gifts to become the best version of myself. Please free me from any distractions that hinder my prayer life, whether they be financial, emotional, physical, mental, spiritual, carnal, social, or professional. These distractions prevent me from maintaining my daily discipline of prayer in my secret place. I seek to practice good self-discipline to become more like Jesus. Please gently transition me from a sense of duty to relishing the sheer joy of daily communion with You. Help me grow, little by little, in spiritual disciplines. I pray this in the strong name of Jesus Christ. Amen.*

4

From Lip Service to Life Change

In our spiritual journey, few practices can propel us as swiftly and profoundly as fasting. When we fast, we do so before Almighty God, not just to abstain from food, but to forge deeper connections with Him. It is more than a ritual; it is a powerful act of faith that breaks strongholds and paves the way for breakthroughs. As we deny our physical needs temporarily, we heighten our spiritual senses, opening ourselves to clearer guidance and renewed strength from above.

In the early nineties, at The School of Large Church Management, C. Peter Wagner taught us on the power of intercession. My prayer life took a radical upturn when I realized Christians were the target, but pastors and their families were the bull's eye of satanic attack. I traveled home determined to seek prayer partners. God gave me right at fifty as will be discussed. Not surprisingly, fasting was the rarest of all spiritual disciplines. Occasionally, I dabbled in this discipline, but like so many other Christians, fasting was something I could take or leave. Until. This. A true House of Prayer *and* Fasting transformed my life and ministry after spending a week with Adalberto and Ninéye Herrera's growing *Casa de Oración* church in Cali, Columbia. As will be seen, fasting unleashes God's miracle-working power like no other spiritual discipline. Let me tell what I learned.

> **Prayer Response:** *Dear Lord, as I embark on this journey, please open new horizons for my faith. Unleash for me the spiritual possibilities that extraordinary prayer and fasting can offer. Guide me, teach me, and show me the way. I pray this in Your name. Amen.*

How to Untap Spiritual Possibilities

What might happen if we added fasting to our times of united prayer? Would the breakthroughs we seek come sooner? Why didn't I see the necessity of both praying *and* fasting? In my last pastorate, I called a church in crisis to fervent, round-the-clock prayer. I now wonder whether fasting might have made the difference in the eyes of Jesus (Mark 9:29). In Bible versions that followed the King James, the word "fasting" is often omitted or relegated to a footnote. I overlooked this spiritual discipline for years, and regretfully, I may never know what might have been.

Pastor Corey Jones, a man whose church truly is a house of prayer, once blogged, "Jesus was effortless, barely breaking a sweat when He healed the sick, miraculously fed thousands, cast out demons, and even raised the dead. But when Jesus prayed, He travailed, staying up through the night, often fasting, and praying with loud cries, even to the point of sweating drops of blood. Maybe we aren't effortlessly reproducing the ministry of Jesus because we aren't exerting ourselves in prayer and fasting like He did."

Fasting, when combined with prayer, offers a unique and powerful spiritual discipline that many throughout history have found transformative. This practice, rooted in biblical tradition, is more than just abstaining from food; it is an intentional act of focusing your mind and spirit on connecting with God. By removing distractions and discomfort, fasting can heighten your sense of God's presence and open you up to spiritual insights and breakthroughs that might otherwise remain out of reach.

When you fast, you're making a conscious choice to prioritize your spiritual life over physical needs, demonstrating a deep commitment and vulnerability before God. This act of devotion can lead to numerous spiritual benefits not the least of which includes:

1. Clarity and insight into situations, revealing solutions and paths previously unseen.

2. Aligning your desires more closely with God's will and empowering you to overcome significant challenges.

3. Opening your heart and mind to new possibilities and opportunities.

4. Helping to demolish formidable barriers (spiritual strongholds), paving the way for freedom and healing.

5. Actively seeking God's intervention and presence in your life and the life of your church.

Remember, the goal of fasting is not simply to abstain from food but to draw closer to God, aligning your heart with His and opening yourself up to the amazing results that occur when prayer and fasting come together.

> **Prayer Response:** *Father, fasting is a discipline I have not practiced extensively, primarily because I enjoy eating. However, I open my heart to Your guidance regarding the integration of fasting with my prayers. Reveal to me the spiritual potential that fasting holds, a potential that could elevate my prayer life to new heights and unlock doors that have previously been closed to me. Teach me not only how to pray but also how to fast and pray. I ask this in Jesus' name. Amen.*

Your Secret Source of Power

In the practice of fasting, the focus should be on sincere connection with God rather than outward appearances, as emphasized in Matthew 6:16, NLT: *"When you fast, don't make it obvious, as the hypocrites do, for they try to look miserable and disheveled so people will admire them for their fasting."* Jentezen Franklin further illuminates this spiritual discipline, stating, "When you eliminate food from your diet for a number of days, your spirit becomes uncluttered by the things of the world and amazingly sensitive to the things of God." Together, these perspectives remind us that true fasting is an internal journey towards spiritual sensitivity and authenticity, away from worldly distractions and the pursuit of others' admiration.

I did not call people to fast because fasting was not one of my regular spiritual disciplines. One of my personal rules of leadership has always been: never ask your followers to do something you are unwilling to do yourself. The truth is, I love food and enjoy eating. I might have missed a meal and called it fasting a few times during the first decade of my ministry. Besides, isn't prayer the primary focus? Fasting? I could take it or leave it. The concept of fasting for spiritual reasons was elusive to me for years, despite this practice being a fundamental aspect of one's relationship with God. After all, Jesus did say, "When you fast," not "if you fast." It's less optional than it may appear.

Dave Williams advised, "Fast if you desire, but it's not mandatory." However, if "leading a fasted life increases our ability to hear from God, walk in His ways, and do His will," why not give it a try?[1] Like many overweight Americans, I typically prefer three square meals a day, which is why I largely left fasting untested and untried, to my own spiritual detriment. Fasting is a "secret source of power" that is often overlooked. It sharpens the mind and enhances sensitivity towards God. Nevertheless, it must be undertaken with a spiritual purpose or intent. If fasting lacks personal significance for you, it is likely to be of little importance to God as well.

---

1 Dave Williams, "The Miracle Results of Fasting", (Tulsa: Harrison House, 2004).

When fasting is practiced with the right motive, it can take your prayer life to the next level. There is no "one-size-fits-all" approach to fasting. It has physical benefits, potentially even health advantages, but it also requires a focus on faith. Fasting is deeply personal and always an act of discipline and self-control.[2] I invite you think about the principle of prayer and fasting to aid in the release of God's power in your life. So, begin to ask God to expand your understanding, as you study what the Bible says about the effectiveness of prayer and fasting.

Prayer Response: *Lord, as I contemplate a time of fasting, fill me with your strength. Help me to use this as a time of growth, renewal, and healing. Calm my anxiety about the discomfort I might face if I give up eating a meal. Provide me with assurance that You will strengthen me during the difficult times and meet me for sweet moments of spiritual growth and surrender. Help me focus not on what is being taken away, but what I'm gaining as I use this as a spiritual discipline. With you leading, Holy Spirit, I am ready. In Jesus' name. Amen.*[3]

Why Motivation Counts

In Zechariah 7:5, NLT, God asks a soul-searching question *"Was it really for me that you were fasting?"* challenging His people to examine the true intentions behind their spiritual practices. Fasting is a powerful practice that deepens and strengthens one's relationship with God. It encourages a commitment to genuine spiritual connection, potentially enriching one's spiritual journey through sincere dedication and purpose.

In this passage from Zechariah, God questions the sincerity and motivation behind their fasts, which should have been times dedicated to prayer and repentance. Instead, they were meant to introspect, uncover any remaining unconfessed sins, and repent for them. Reflecting on this during Lent, I began to question whether my own motivations

---

2 Healthy Hildegard, "Spiritual Fasting: a Practice of Mind, Body, & Spirit,"
3 Gleaned from Sara, "The 5 Best Prayers for Fasting," The Holy Mess, October 1, 2021.

were misguided. While I understand the importance of spiritual disciplines, my actions may not have aligned with this understanding.

For instance, on Day 5 of a recent Lenten calendar, we were encouraged to "choose one thing to begin fasting." My grandchildren opted to give up desserts and sodas. When they asked me what I would be fasting from, I chose to give up my "No Sugar Added" ice cream due to my diabetes.

Honestly, I lacked a spiritual purpose or focus for my fast. If it held little significance for me, it likely held even less significance for God. Thus, I abandoned my fast midway through Lent. As Jentezen Franklin wisely cautions, "The way you approach your fast is extremely important. If you are not serious about it, then you won't achieve meaningful results. The more serious you are about the fast, the more seriously God will respond."[4] If you approach fasting with frivolity or a lighthearted attitude, it risks becoming a meaningless religious routine. My heart truly wasn't invested in the fast. Engaging in activities suggested on a laminated church Lenten calendar, without genuine commitment, may be a good exercise in discipline, but for me, it lacked spiritual depth. However, when my motivation was to draw closer to God, every time I fasted, I felt a deeper connection with Him. He is our greatest reward.

If your primary motivation for fasting is spiritual—namely, to nourish your faith—you can seek His blessings for yourself and others, and your faith will be strengthened. Brittany Yesudasan emphasizes, "It's important to understand that fasting is not a way to get a better response to prayer. Rather, true fasting is a means of fostering a better (humbler) approach to prayer."

If you plan to fast, consider this question: Why am I fasting? Turn your answer into a prayer.

Prayer Response: *Father, your Word declares that fasting is a biblical way to truly humble myself before You. King David said, "I humbled myself with fasting" (Psalm*

---
[4] Quotes from Franklin, Fasting Journal (Lake Mary: Charisma House, 2008) 2.

35:13, NKJV). *I ask you Holy Spirit to examine my motives because I now understand that if it doesn't mean much to me, it probably means very little to You. Reveal my true spiritual condition and may it result in brokenness, repentance, and a transformed life. Strengthen my confidence and faith in You. Enable me to feel mentally, spiritually, and physically refreshed. This I pray, in Jesus' name. Amen.*[5]

The Mother of All Fasts

In Matthew 4:1-2, NIV, we see the powerful example of Jesus: *"Then Jesus was led by the Spirit into the wilderness to be tempted by the devil. After fasting forty days and forty nights, he was hungry."* This passage highlights not only the physical challenge of fasting but also its role in spiritual preparation and testing. Arthur Wallis provides a thoughtful caution on the practice of extended fasting: "One would need to be very sure of the leading of God to undertake such a fast for any period longer than three days." Together, these perspectives emphasize the importance of divine guidance and discernment when embarking on significant fasting periods, reminding us that such deep spiritual endeavors should be approached with care and a clear sense of purpose.

Matthew delivers one of the greatest understatements in the Bible in chapter 4, verse 2. Right after His baptism, Jesus was led by the Spirit into the desert to be tempted by the devil. Similarly, Moses was in the presence of the Lord for consecutive forty-day fasts, "neither eating bread nor drinking water" (Exodus 34:28; Deuteronomy 9:9, 18). These were *absolute* fasts that would likely be fatal for most people today without supernatural intervention and should probably never be attempted without water. The duration of an absolute fast often correlates with the level of desperation involved. For instance, when Queen Esther understood the severe threat of genocide facing the entire Jewish race, she called for a three-day absolute fast (Esther 4:16). As Arthur

---

[5] Adapted from Brittany Yesudasan, "What is Biblical Fasting and Does It Work?" Train and Grow.

Wallis notes, "Desperate situations require desperate measures. When undertaken with a pure heart and right motives, fasting can serve as a key to unlock doors where other methods have failed."[6]

Always consult your physician before undertaking any fast that exceeds three days. Only a select few should attempt the mother of all fasts—forty days—without thorough preparation and potential medical supervision. Maximum caution and medical safety are strongly recommended. If you have underlying health conditions such as pregnancy, anemia, behavioral disorders, or other chronic health problems, consult your physician before considering any fast.[7] Nonetheless, one of my church planters, Roland Hearn, an Australian by birth, along with Texas layman Brad Mercer, undertook a forty-day fast in preparation for launching a new church in Frisco, Texas. They believed that fasting was essential before starting this new venture. "Planting a church is a challenging endeavor," said Roland, who found the cultural differences "next to terrifying."[8] Their incredible story follows.

> **Prayer Response:** *Lord, this whole idea of fasting is foreign to me. Jesus, You fasted before You began Your public ministry (Luke 4:1,2). I am hungry for You, and I feel You are drawing me to this discipline. The early church fasted while worshiping and committing their ministry to the Lord. They also sought the Lord through fasting for guidance when they appointed leaders (Acts 13:2; 14:23). Please confirm to me the type of fast You're asking me to undertake. I am ready to humble myself before You that my faith and confidence in You may be strengthened. Amen.*

Fasting to Conquer Fear of Failure

Roland Hearn's reflection, "While personally I am always excited by new adventures, the thought of failure created significant fear for

---
6 Quotes from Arthur Wallis, God's Chosen Fast (Fort Washington: CLC Publications, 1968) 19.
7 Brittany Yesudasan, "What is Biblical Fasting, and Does It Work?" Cru, Train & Grow.
8 Unidentified quotes are from information provided by Rev. Roland Hearn, District Superintendent Australia North and West Church of the Nazarene.

me," resonates with common human experiences. It highlights the tension between the excitement of new endeavors and the fear of failure. Together, these insights remind us to anchor our courage and confidence in God's unwavering support as we navigate the challenges and opportunities before us.

The church planters aimed to discern the best path to reach a new community. Tasked with launching a Nazarene church in Frisco, TX, a prospering area, they were anxious about the unknown and potential failure. Fear often stems from the possibility of making mistakes, looking foolish, or not meeting expectations—in other words, the fear of failure.[9] Kristen Feola notes, "Fear can be a crippling emotion, often keeping us from moving forward when the Lord wants us to step out in faith."[10]

Roland and Brad believed that fasting would help them reframe their fears before embarking on their mission, thereby reducing stress and anxiety. Fasting prepared their hearts as they sought God's direction, clarified their motives, and focused their vision for the church. Fasting isn't a way to manipulate God into guaranteeing success but provides "a unique opportunity to know God in a deeper way and to hear His voice more clearly." Kristen Feola explains: "When you fast, you deny yourself food, or certain foods, for a specified period as an act of surrender and worship. Those who have participated in this spiritual discipline can testify to experiencing an increased sensitivity to the Holy Spirit, greater awareness of their dependence on the Lord, and a stronger compulsion to intercede for others."[11] As we will discover Roland and Brad opened their hearts to the grace of God, allowing His love to flow more fully through them to the community around them. Fasting reminded them of their dependence on God and His grace.

Prayer Response: *Mighty God, I bring all my fears and anxieties to you, asking for divine protection. Give me courage to surrender my fears into your capable hands.*

---

9 Susan Peppercorn, "How to Overcome Your Fear of Failure," Harvard Business Review, December 10, 2018.
10 Kristen Feola, "How to Overcome Your Fear of Fasting," Zondervan blog, February 20, 2012.
11 Ibid.

Shield me from every form of harm and danger that often paralyze me with fear. Strengthen my faith because your Word says You have not given me the spirit of fear but of power, love, and a sound mind. You, Lord, are my refuge and fortress.[12] *Now fill me with Your peace. In Jesus' name. Amen.*

Fasting Factors

Fasting is a means to seek divine guidance and protection, acknowledging our reliance on God in times of need. Fasting that achieves a spiritual purpose, denies and masters the appetite, and manifests an earnest desire to seek God, emphasizes the transformative power of fasting. It involves disciplining the body and expressing a sincere yearning for God's presence and guidance. Together, these thoughts invite us to consider fasting not just as a physical act but as a profound spiritual discipline that aligns our hearts with God's will and purposes.

Roland and Brad were convinced that a 40-day fast would "more fully open their hearts to the grace of God." When we fast, we are reminded of our dependence upon God and His grace. They believed fasting would allow God's love to "more fully embrace them and therefore flow through their lives to the people in the community around them." Fasting not only benefits the individual but also has significant positive impacts on the lives of others, demonstrating its social and transpersonal benefits.

"Fasting is also a way the Lord invites us into a deeper relationship with Him and it's a way to declare to yourself and to Christ that you want more of what He has for you." Shanna Schutte also teaches, "Fasting is a way of saying, 'Lord, I believe you will speak to me, and I am making room for you to do so.'"[13] The planters certainly made room for God to speak.

Spiritual, practical, and physical parameters—prayer, reading, and extensive conversations about their hopes and goals—had to be de-

---

12 David Small, "21 Best Prayers to Overcome Fear," The Prayer Warrior, May 18, 2023.
13 Shanna Schutte, "The Blessings of Fasting," Wisdom Hunters, March 20, 2022.

veloped. They chose to drink only water, freshly juiced fruit, and vegetables: no tea, coffee, sodas or purchased juices. They began each day with a drink of freshly juiced fruit and ended each day with a drink of water that had vegetables boiling in it for enough time to leach out the nutrients. They studied the physical ramifications of their fast.

Once their bodies had used the excess fat, they would begin to experience starvation. Consuming natural vitamins and minerals extended the time it would take to get to that critical point. In a 40-day fast you experience hunger for the first few days, reduced discomfort for an unspecified period, and then extreme discomfort as the body enters the first stages of starvation. It was at that point that I advised Roland and Brad to cease the fast. If not, to modify it. Before you embark on an extended fast, you must ask the Lord for direction on how your body will be sustained for the duration of the fast.

> **Prayer Response:** *God, the time of my fast is coming to an end. Thank you for giving me the strength to carry this out. I have grown in strength and in my relationship with You. I know I could never have done this by my own power. Lead and guide me in my next steps. Help me move slowly and gently back into my regular routine. In Jesus name I ask this, Amen*[14]

Deepening our Connection with God

If you're aiming to pursue a deeper connection with God and gain a clearer understanding of His will, fasting can serve as a powerful expression of your desire for more of what God offers. Engaging in fasting with purpose and intent underscores your longing to connect with Him and align your life with His plans.

Together, these insights encourage us to ensure that our fasting and spiritual disciplines are heartfelt expressions of our devotion to God, rather than mere rituals, and to use them as opportunities to deepen our relationship with Him and seek His guidance in our lives. Shanna

---
14 Adapted from Sara, "5 Best Prayers for Fasting," The Holy Mess, April 11, 2023.

Schutte reiterates that "When we fast, we align ourselves with God in a way that acknowledges He is the Lord, and that we are not." Zechariah is told to ask what good is achieved to go through a religious routine, however strict, if you have no intention to obey (Zech. 7:5). And God reproves them for it. Their fasting wasn't approved by God. Something was missing. Form without power (2 Tim. 3:5)? Discipline or duty, but no life, passion, or authenticity. Religious routine must never be about pleasing ourselves while refusing to honor God and His Word.

If you just hope to impress God by your fasting, and gain a little oomph for your prayers, it will not work. The priests were hard on themselves for all the wrong reasons. God desires more than simply going through the motions however well-intended. Fasting for the wrong motives gets us nowhere with God (Isa. 58:4-7). We cannot win God's approval by what we eat or don't eat (1 Cor. 8:8). "We don't lose anything if we don't eat it, and we don't gain anything if we do." What impresses God is heart change that issues in life change.

Few of us are asked to go above and beyond as Roland and Brad did in their 40-day fast. Spiritual disciplines done with the right motives reap amazing rewards (see Matt.6). The spiritual benefits and blessings of an extended fast are incalculable. Brooke Obie summarizes the spiritual benefits: "Fasting is less about what we're giving up and much more about what we're making room for. When we fast, we exchange what we need to survive for what we need to live—more of God."[15]

> **Prayer Response:** *Forgive me, Lord, for craving anything more than you. Please redirect my hunger. Open my eyes to the benefits of fasting. Open my heart to you like never before. Give me the desire to turn to you with all my heart, with all my soul and with all my strength. When I am tempted to quit this fast, please show me the way out that you promise in Your Word. I am clinging to that promise right now (1 Cor. 10:13). I want to follow through on my intentions and most of all, Father, I want*

---
15 Brooke Obie, "5 Spiritual Benefits of Fasting," Guideposts website.

to bring You glory and honor. I know I can do all things through Christ who gives me strength (Phil. 4:13).[16]

Transformative Fasting

In a time when normal life had been completely disrupted, Ezra records that they fasted and fervently prayed for God's guidance and intervention both in their lives and in the community He called him to serve, and He listened to their prayers (Ezra 8:23). Ezra's call for a fast was for the protection of God's people as they fulfilled their mission. These devoted church planters fasted and prayed with purpose.

The fasting experience for Brad was virtually textbook: initial hunger and mild discomfort until about day 34, followed by increased pain. He was "so close to the end, he pushed through until the 40th day." Roland experienced significant discomfort throughout the entire fast. His pain got noticeably intense the last couple of days.

My well-intentioned friends each lost over 25 lbs. Emaciated, literally skin and bones, they were beyond serious about seeking the face of God. With no energy to spare, they prayer-walked the streets of the Frisco community for an hour each day burning calories they couldn't afford to lose. Fasting made them "extraordinarily aware of God's work in their own lives." By fasting, they meditated and cleansed their souls hoping to receive more of the Holy Spirit and become more empowered to serve Christ in this new mission.

God had melded their hearts to a high and lofty purpose. They were fasting with the right mindset. A dream emerged through fasting that only God could make possible. Success is never guaranteed. As their district superintendent, I cheered them on and did everything humanly possible to support the fledgling new start. If we thought all their fasting would guarantee smashing success, that probably bordered on manipulation of God. Fasting should never be used as a tactic to manipulate God, as it suggests a misguided belief that we can control Him through our actions. Natalie Nichols warns that attempting

---
16 Scriptural parts adapted from Sara, "5 Best Prayers for Fasting."

to "twist God's arm" through fasting elevates our desires above His, making us the rulers of our lives. She emphasizes that fasting should lead to transformation within ourselves, not in God, highlighting that the true purpose of fasting and prayer is to change us, not to force God's hand.[17]

> **Prayer Response:** *Father, I ask in Jesus' name that You would fill me afresh with the wonder of Your love and power. Help me to discern when to rest, when to feast, and how to actively engage my faith as I wait for You to breakthrough. Help me to lose my taste for worldly things that weaken me and acquire a taste for those things that strengthen me. Empower me to make the necessary changes. Amen.*

A Fasting Epiphany

The parable of not pouring new wine into old wineskins (Matt. 9:17), illustrates the necessity for change and adaptation, much like Roland Hearn's insight on relinquishing control to God. Hearn emphasizes the importance of allowing God to be God, rather than attempting to assume His role or expecting Him to merely solve personal problems. Both thoughts highlight the need for openness to transformation and trust in God's wisdom.

Fasting breaks the power of the flesh and brings our faith to a whole new level. Focusing on God and becoming more attentive to Him were reasons why Roland and Brad denied physical gratifications during their fast. Their flesh was brought into subjection to the Spirit that they might become more attentive to God and sensitive to Him—and the purpose of the fast was accomplished. Roland longed for supernatural blessings to be released and the power of God to make an eternal impact. Instead, the results were puzzling.

---

[17] Natalie Nichols, "Fasting is Not Twisting God's Arm," Shades of Grace Ministries, January 30, 2017.

"In the months following the fast," he recalls, "progress on the New Start was very slow." He "came face to face with his fear of failure and it pushed him to the breaking point." The old wineskin burst from the pressure. He collapsed under the weight of it all and had to be hospitalized. Not the result anyone was hoping for.

Broken and spilled out on his back in a hospital bed, Roland experienced what he described as "an epiphany" that "moved his understanding of the grace of God to an unshakeable awareness of His sufficiency." He journaled words that are indelibly etched on the walls of his memory twenty-plus years ago: *"God must be God, and love must be enough."* The new wine of love would be his only vehicle of influence in the lives of those he was trying to reach. Fasting changed Roland not God. "I must love people adequately enough for them to experience love. I had no other way of influencing people that was consistent with the grace of God." He discovered the truth of Natalie Nichols words: "Fasting is not making God do something He doesn't want to do. It is positioning yourself and preparing your heart for what God wants to do in you."[18]

Prayer Response: *Lord Jesus, here I am again, asking You to do what only You can do in my life. I ask You for a fresh vision for what breakthrough will look like in my life. Help me to pursue healing while I wait for my miracle. Show me how to rest right in the middle of the storm. Help me to enjoy the feast You prepare for me, right in the middle of the battlefield. I want my whole life to testify that there's a God in heaven who knows my name and who will get me safely home. Scripture tells me that You are the same yesterday, today, and forever. You are the God who performs miracles! So do a miracle in me! Heal me through and through! Amen.*

---

18 Ibid.

From Breakdown to Breakthrough

Do you think that God arranges every situation for the benefit of those who love Him and align with His purpose, as stated in Romans 8:28? I trust in God's sovereign power to integrate every aspect of our lives into a broader plan for good. Personal experiences frequently demonstrate how God's timing and guidance help us understand His will. By continually trusting in God's flawless plan, He will reveal how the events in our lives foster spiritual development and help us align with His intentions.

As the Lord so often does, He works in ways we perceive as unthinkably bad, to achieve the very good our fasting envisions. During his hospital stay, Roland met a young man named Christopher who became the first recipient of his rekindled love. He led him to Christ, and Chris moved into a deep relationship with God and became a board member of the church that was planted a few weeks later. As Roland reflected on his journey and the friendships forged through trials and shared faith, he recognized that these relationships were among the most profound and enduring of his life. Each member of his church circle had become instrumental in one another's lives, offering support, understanding, and encouragement rooted in a shared divine connection. This story from his life is a testament to the transformative power of faith and community in the face of adversity.

It wasn't the fast, but what came after this mother of all fasts. Roland is profoundly convinced "the fast allowed him to see the deeply flawed way he processed his place in the Kingdom of God." The fast "laid the foundation for the revelation of God's love." Fasting can be transformational. Fasting brought "spiritual clarity, renewed faith, and more energy within the context of grace." It is not surprising that many people experienced transformation in their lives. So transformational was that fast in Roland's life that a few years ago he started an annual ritual of fasting for the month of October called *Oktoberfast* and uses the same fasting formula he used all those years ago.

Prayer Response: *Lord, use your miracle-working power to bring a breakthrough in my life. Fill me afresh with the wonder of Your love and power. I am determined to win this battle with [fill in your area of greatest need]. Help me to discern when to rest, when to feast, and how to actively engage my faith as I wait for You to breakthrough. May my life display Your power. Do the impossible in and through me, I pray.*[19] *May I know your all-conquering power, today, Lord. You have loved me and have freed me from my sins by your blood. To you be glory and power forever and ever. Through Jesus Christ our Lord, Amen.*

Three Compelling Lessons

Roland's friend, Brad passed away over a decade ago, but what they learned became very clear when I asked him to summarize three compelling lessons from their fasting season:

1. "God must be God and love must be enough." Love must be the motivation of all our efforts. Is your love self-generated or God-initiated? Nothing is more fundamental than *agape* love (see Rom.5:5). "Love, then, is the chief motivation for a life of Christian service and good works."[20] When we love God, we will want to glorify God, please God, and know God better. Compassion becomes love in action and takes us well beyond surface Christianity.

2. "God's grace during circumstances is more about transforming me than it is about transforming the circumstances. When we are transformed to become more like Jesus, we begin to relate to our circumstances from His perspective. From there, things look different, and the wisdom of how to respond flows from His love." We have zero control over our circumstances but 100 percent control over our perspective on those circumstances. Roland's focus changed from inward to upward to outward, enabling him to focus

---
19 Adapted from Susie Larson, in "Fasting Prayers for Powerful Revelation and Breakthrough," Bible Study Tools, January 16, 2023.
20 Gracelife website, "The Christian's Motivation for Serving God," May 2010.

on what God was doing, not on his circumstances. Where is your focus?

3. "The ever-present truth that Jesus Christ is still building His Kingdom, His message matters, and He makes a difference." Roland's perspective on his role in ministry changed too. He learned to walk beside Christ as He transforms lives. Roland was ready to respond however God might choose to answer his prayers. Remember the words of John Wesley: "Fasting is only a way which God has ordained, wherein we wait for His unmerited mercy; and wherein, without any deservedness of our own, He has promised to freely give us His blessing."

Prayer Response: *"Christ with me, Christ before me, Christ behind me, Christ in me, Christ beneath me, Christ above me, Christ on my right, Christ on my left, Christ when I lie down, Christ when I sit down, Christ when I arise, Christ in the heart of every man (woman) who thinks of me, Christ in the mouth of everyone who speaks of me, Christ in every eye that sees me, Christ in every ear that hears me." —A prayer of St. Patrick*

The Tipping Point

Across cultures and religions, fasting has served as a fundamental way to communicate with the Divine, reflecting a universal practice of spiritual devotion and connection. Embracing both sacrifice and dedication can deepen our spiritual journey and alignment with God's will.

Fasting could be the one thing lacking. Jesus told the rich, young ruler that he lacked one thing—give to the poor and come follow Him. Regrettably, he refused. Some of our greatest breakthroughs are missed because we fail to pray *and* fast. Prayers of intercession for God to break every stronghold, demolish arguments and every pretension that sets itself up against the knowledge of God; that every thought be taken captive in obedience to Christ (2 Corinthians 10:5) are wrestling prayers. "Fasting intersects with and intensifies prayer" by showing "sincere intention" and increasing the urgency of our prayers to say nothing about amplifying the frequency and focus of our praying.[21]

Fasting with wrestling prayer enables us to "push through all the difficulties and obstacles; drive back all the opposing forces of Satan; and secure the will of God" (Small). Hungry people are desperate people. Fasting shows God how serious we are. "Every time you feel a hunger pang, reflect and/or pray about your purpose" (McKay). Julio C. Ruibal discovered; "Our greatest victories are won on our knees and with empty stomachs." Regardless of the outcome, fasting brings us into "a deeper, more intimate, and more powerful relationship with the Lord," the very thing we want and need the most. Fr. Thomas Ryan put it succinctly, fasting is "a wellspring for the spiritually dry, a compass for the spiritually lost, and inner nourishment for the spiritually hungry."[22]

Ask God if He might be calling you to rediscover the biblical practice of fasting. "Every time you feel hungry, instead of reaching for food, use the moment to engage with why you're fasting" (McKay). Yes, Lord, renew my contact with You.

> **Prayer Response:** *Lord, I ask You to make my prayer and fasting times of sowing into the Spirit. If I continue to sow in prayer, the day will come when there is a tipping point. Lord, I've been praying about [insert your greatest need here] over and over, for weeks, months, or even years. I pray the tipping point will happen soon and that thing will come to pass. Please allow me to see it with my own eyes. Prayers are powerful, they change things. Help me never to stop praying and give up. I won't quit praying. I won't stop standing in faith for those things I am believing for! Amen.*[23]

---

21 Quoted in Brett and Kate McKay, "The Spiritual Disciplines: Fasting," The Art of Manliness.com.
22 Thomas Ryan, The Sacred Art of Fasting, from Amazon promo, chapter 9.
23 Gleaned from Kim, "Tipping Points...Continued," A New Thing Ministries.

Between a Rock and the Red Sea

It is difficult not to be unsettled, perpetually uncertain and honestly, unbelieving, when circumstances have us between a rock and the Red Sea (see Exodus 14:13-14). We know how intertwined fear, anxiety, and worry can be. The global rampage of Covid 19, drew thousands of people to fasting and prayer, calling on God for divine intervention. We found ourselves at the same place as God's people when caught between the pursuing Egyptian hostiles and the Red Sea. It's incredibly difficult to stand still, do nothing and stay calm having referred everything to God's intervention (1 Pet.5:7). When crisis squeezes us to the water's edge, it's incredibly difficult to maintain calm and believe God's got this! If we say we trust in God, we fear Him because we know that He can summon legions of angels to the battlefield and sometimes we just get to stand and watch Him fight the battle only He can win.

The Lord of Heaven's Armies showed up to fight for His people. Refuse to believe Satan's lies and fall into sin and despair that will immobilize you in fear and rob your peace. Hear again the Lord's command to Moses: "Fear not, I AM [is] fighting for you." Remember, When God is involved, the equation always results in a supermajority. His name is the solution to every problem and anxiety. His name is the answer to every question and doubt. His presence calms every fear, seals every prayer, and wins every battle. Calm your fears by casting or throwing all your anxiety at His feet. The longer you hold to on your fears, the more anxious you will be. Face your fears and watch them fade. Tell Him what makes you anxious and let it go in prayer today.

Prayer Response: *Lord God, Moses told your people to stand still and watch how You would rescue them, and the waters parted. At times, Jesus, my fear is racing ahead of my logic and at times it is downright irrational. I cry out to You. You told your disciples "be not afraid" and their trust, though imperfect, empowered them to do great things in your name. Soothe my fears, anxieties, and cares. I throw them down at Your feet [name them one by* *one]. Give me the power to wait and see Your salvation, or courage to step out of the boat into the unknown. I pray in the name of the one who rescued Peter when his fear got the better of him, Jesus Christ my Lord. Amen.*[24]

God's Track Record of Faithfulness

In times of challenge and uncertainty, stand firm and trust in the Lord's deliverance. Embrace stillness and unwavering faith, and you will witness God's power and faithfulness in your life. The Lord has a message for God-fearers. Don't put your trust in idols or any substitute! Idols cannot speak, see, hear, smell, or feel (Psalm 115:5-8). They cannot walk or talk. They're dead and useless. *"I, on the other hand, can do all of these things and more,"* says our trustworthy God. Trust in the Lord! The psalmist singles out two groups of hearers: leaders and God-fearers. It's not more trying but trusting that God wants. He *"remembers you and will bless you."*

Trust God's track record of faithfulness found in His Word to help inform and define your own faith. "When you see faith in the Bible, it is based on a relationship with God. You see, Israel did not have to blindly jump out into the Red Sea. They had seen God act in the past."[25] This should give us confidence in God's future blessing. He has not forgotten us in the past and He is not about to forget us in the future! Don't just try harder. Trust more. If we trust without ceasing and pray without ceasing the Lord has promised to bless us without ceasing. Are you in a difficult place right now? God-fearers place their trust and keep on trusting because of God's past performance of faithfulness. We are witnesses to a watching world.

He has blessed us in the past. He will bless us in the present and in the future. Stand in faith even when you're having the hardest time of your life. Don't let your circumstances block your view of God. The level of our difficulties may differ, but with God as our Helper and

---

[24] Adapted from Beth Hargrave, "Fasting from Worry and Fear (Day 3)," Cross Life Lutheran Church, March 29, 2019.
[25] Quotes from Jonathan Srock, "God's Track Record," July 10, 2019.

Shield, victory is assured! You say you trust in God, now show it. Ask God to show you what needs to change in your attitude and perspective. Confess your helplessness without Him. Pray your confidence: "I can do all things through Christ who strengthens me" (Phil.4:13, KJV). This is our holy confidence as we fast and pray.

> **Prayer Response:** *Dear Lord, give me the courage to face my fears and doubts. Enable me to see past my weaknesses and challenges so that I may have the confidence to take charge of my life. Grant me a strong sense of faith in You, knowing that You will always be there with me as I step out into the unknown. Help me to trust in Your guidance and grace so that I can feel secure in every moment of life. Thank You for Your help and strength. In Jesus Name. Amen.*[26]

---

26 Daniel, Prayer Warrior, "5 Powerful Prayers for Confidence," January 29, 2023

5

Accessing the Miraculous

> *"When fasting is added to your prayers they become an extreme in-your-face statement to the devil. He gets disturbed and defeated often through distraction, because he knows fasting releases God's power."*
>
> –Jentezen Franklin paraphrase

The back story of this chapter was a life-transforming trip with twenty-three people from Southern Florida to Cali, Colombia, the home of a church that lived up to its name: *Casa de Oración* (House of Prayer). For seven days we sat under the anointed instruction of Adalberto and Ninéye Herrera and members of their staff. I had believed in and practiced the power of prayer, but as I've already admitted, I only dabbled in the discipline of fasting. Something changed in Cali. We experienced the power of prayer *and* fasting up-close and personal. Faith, prayer, and fasting are interconnected and mutually supportive. Fasting enhances the effectiveness of prayer and faith, allowing both to develop and grow fully, and together they can lead to remarkable outcomes.

> **Prayer Response:** *Lord, I desire to grow and develop in my walk with You. I am growing in my walk with You. If fasting will take me deeper and draw me closer to You, grant me the grace to dive into this discipline with a willing heart. I desire Your divine power in my life, and I now ask You to teach me how to fast in a way that fits me physically, and outfits me spiritually in ways I have not yet considered. In Your Powerful Name. Amen.*

The Transformative Power of Prayer and Fasting

Nearly two decades ago, I discovered of the power of fasting on that weeklong trip to the sprawling city of Cali, Colombia, the same city where more than 50,000 people gathered for an all-night prayer service after the martyrdom of Julio C. Ruibal, the catalyst for prayer and unity in the city. In the months following that city-wide prayer-meeting, God began dismantling the Cali drug cartels, transforming the city, one strategic person at a time. We were there to observe and absorb everything we could learn about one of the fastest growing churches in the Church of the Nazarene that had rocketed past 1,000 to 7,000 with no leveling off in sight.

Thousands of cars speed by the *Casa de Oración* church day and night. Jesus' words imprinted on the wall of the church greet passersby: *"Come to me, all who labor and are heavy laden, and I will give you rest"* (Matt. 11:28, ESV) One busy afternoon, those comforting words caught the eye of Adrianna Rodriquez, and she felt supernaturally drawn to that House of Prayer. She might have zoomed past; but instead, she attended service the very next day and was saved.

Prayer and fasting draws people who desperately need help to a rendezvous with God. It opens doors for the Gospel that might have otherwise remained closed. Prayer (and fasting) opens the door for witnessing and softens hearts for receptiveness. Adding fasting to your prayers may be the difference between defeat or victory. Fasting gives the Lord our full attention and prayer asks him to be at work as we evangelize. Helene Nsin Oum submits, "Combining prayer with fasting connects the natural to the supernatural."[1] I challenge you to fast a meal this week and use the time to pray for lost family members (we all have them), friends, or neighbors.

> **Prayer Response:** *Loving Shepherd of the lost sheep, I pray for [my loved one] to know you. I pray for eyes to be opened to see, ears to hear, and a heart to know you. Crack open the door, break into [his] life and let [her] see a glimmer of your power. Lord, knowing You personally is the greatest, most powerful part of my life and I desire this for [everyone else in my life]. I pray for [my loved one] to know You and be enlightened to the hope found in You. So, Lord, break through and open [his] eyes to you, speak into [her] heart, and help [him] see your glory. Amen.*[2]

"The Other Side of Yes"

The Cali church introduced Adrianna Rodriquez to the One who invited her to come—to a Person not a program. She found herself in a safe place—she didn't know anyone, and no one knew her, but she felt welcomed and loved by people who accepted her and loved her unconditionally. She heard the Gospel preached for the first time, and when the invitation to respond was given, she went forward along with other seekers to accept Christ as her personal Savior. Adrianna was given a place to belong and to begin living on the other side of yes as a new creation in Christ. She grasped this once-in-a-lifetime opportunity; she committed herself to Christ, and her life suddenly overflowed with new possibilities, amongst them was the chance to become a catalyst for the transformation of her home and family. Transformation is the work of the Holy Spirit. Changing hearts is what God does best.

---

1 Helene Nsin Oum, "Prayer and Fasting for Evangelism," Lausanne World Pulse Archives, 05-2006.
2 Adapted from Kathryn Shirey, "Prayer for a Loved One's Salvation," Prayer Possibilities, October 28, 2019.

Her father-in-law, Gilberto Rodriquez, one of the top six drug lords in the Cali cartel, had been arrested for drug trafficking in a horrific apprehension. An informant had given up his location for $5M in reward money. DEA agents located Gilberto and Adrianna's mother hiding inside of a thick-walled bunker equipped with oxygen tanks and other survival essentials. The agents began drilling through the wall with long drill bits missing on the first attempt but kept drilling, striking Gilberto two times. He finally surrendered or he would die. He was tried and convicted in Miami and sentenced to 30 years in prison.

Dynamic encounters with Jesus profoundly transform individuals from within. Adrianna was on a certain path, yet her encounter with the Living Christ radically altered her life's direction. Fasting unleashes supernatural blessings and God's transformative power. Start by fasting and praying for God to bring at least one new convert to your church. May God assist us in welcoming a new believer this month.

> **Prayer Response:** *Lord, I pray that You would teach me to yield myself to Your Spirit as I pray for the salvation of those who do not know you. Holy Spirit, teach me to trust You as a living person who leads my life and my prayers. I long to see Your power in my life just as the Apostle Paul did as he reached out to the lost (1 Cor. 2:2-5). I thank You that You indwell, seal, sanctify, and empower me. You guide me, teach me, and pray through me. Help me to partner with You as I use Your Word in praying for the salvation of my family, friends, and co-workers [insert names here]. Make me sensitive to Your promptings and teach me to partner with You in praying Your Word over those who are searching for You.[3] In the name of Jesus our only means of salvation, Amen.*

---

3 Adapted from Debbie Przybylski, "A Prayer for the Salvation of Others," Crosswalk.com, October 25, 2018.

All It Takes is One!

Adrianna's personal encounter with Jesus altered the entire trajectory of her life—like a cool, cleansing shower on a hot, sweaty day. God's forgiveness washed away her sin and guilt. Her past was forgiven; her present transformed; her future forever changed. Adrianna's decision to follow Jesus radically transformed her home from a drug haven to a prayer chamber. Her conversion allowed God to rebuild her home with Christ at the heart and center of her family. It took real courage to be the first in her family to accept Christ, but she courageously did so, alone. Adrianna had no idea of "household salvation" (Josh. 24:14.) She personally obeyed God's call and soon after, her husband, Juan Rodriquez, owner of a national soccer team, and each of her children followed her into the faith. Wife, for all you know, you might save your husband. Husband, for all you know, you might save your wife (see 1 Cor.7:16) and together your entire household.

Adrianna didn't simply start to follow Christianity; she followed *Christ!* She responded with no assurance that God would save her entire family. Acts 16:31 came true for Adrianna but is no guarantee that this will always be the case. God gave no promise of a change in the consequences of her father-in-law's sins. What He did offer was eternal life and a relationship with himself. Because of the Cali church's emphasis on prayer and fasting, I must believe her husband, Juan, and her children were on her Top Five Hit List for salvation. She wanted them to hear of God's love and to discover what she had found in Christ.

Adrianna's radically refocused life was a winsome witness that influenced her family. When our hearts are transformed by Christ's love and we are changed by His grace, we have something significant to say about Him (see Acts 4:20). On a 3 X 5 card write your Top Five Hit List for salvation. Pray for them daily. It is never an annoyance to God if you pray for the salvation of your family again and again and again. Never forget, transformational prayer imbues our homes with God's presence and fills its inhabitants with authentic Christ-like attitudes and relationships.

Prayer Response: *Mighty God, I come before you bearing the burden of the sins of my loved ones [name them one by one]. I pray that they may get to know You and know how great You are. Deliver them from the hands of Satan, who has blinded them from seeing the light of the Good News. Open their eyes to see your goodness. Open their minds to understand your sacrifice of your son, Jesus Christ. Forgive them their sins and cleanse them with the mighty blood of your son, Jesus. Be their Savior. Amen.*[4]

Transformational Change

Transformation is achievable. Whatever holds you back can be overcome, allowing you to walk in a newness of heart and life once you embrace the influence of our Lord and Savior's sacrifice.

Team members entered the spacious, high-security estate of Gilberto Rodriquez on that balmy January Friday night. We walked the spacious, well-manicured grounds as we waited for the Bible Study to begin. I imagined the multi-million-dollar drug deals consummated there. Then it hit me. Only God can transform a drug lord's haven into a house of prayer. With the spirit of Satan cast out, the Spirit of God took up residence in that place. God specializes in transforming unholy places into hallowed spaces as we saw in Tyler, Texas (Chapter 2). Holiness happens where the Spirit of God dwells. Through Christ unholy spaces become holy places when dwelt by transformed people.

That night three new attendees at the Bible Study prayed to receive Christ. Adrianna had only been a Christian for one year. She told how "desperate and hopeless" she was when she drove past the *Casa de Oración* church. United, fervent prayer and fasting opens doors in miraculous ways. Seeing the Spirit draw an unsaved family to salvation in the former home of a Cali drug lord was a fresh demonstration of God's power to not only transform unholy places but the people who dwell in them. Positive change doesn't just happen. Transformational change requires a

---

[4] Adapted from ConnectUS, "12 Powerful Prayers for Unsaved Loved Ones," Crosswalk.com, January 29, 2020.

catalyst. Adrianna was the spiritual catalyst. She lived in the gift of God, "and when we live in God's gift," as Doug Reed intimates, "all of life becomes a place where we take off our shoes."[5] Holy places do not make us holy; only the holy person Jesus can make us holy. Desolate, barren lives, destroyed by drugs, alcohol, and brokenness, can be transformed into fruitful, productive lives. This is why we fast and pray! Transformational change pleases God. It pleases God when we see the supernatural results.

> **Prayer Response:** *Almighty God, you are all-powerful, you can do anything you desire. I ask you today to transform my circumstances through your favor and blessing. Cover me with your Holy Spirit, O God. Draw me to greater faith in Him who can do all things. According to Your eternal mercy, establish, strengthen, and reconcile me and my family in Christ. Transform us and permit us to set our minds on things above, according to the revelation of Your Word and Spirit. May grace, mercy, and peace be with us, as we seek your face in truth and love." Change my heart O God… make it ever new…" Through Jesus Christ, our Lord, Amen.*

The Birth of a Vision

Our team was up at 3:52 a.m. to be at the *Casa de Oración* church by 6:00 a.m. for the first prayer meeting of the week. A cacophony of praying saints walked and prayed in what felt like a river of the Spirit. Holy hands were raised high. I will never forget that moving circle of intercessional crying out to God for the lost in their city. Sunrise had not yet ushered in the morning light, yet a vision of the transformative power of prayer and fasting was beginning to blossom. These Cali believers were passionate about unleashing the power of God on their church and community.

Vision is better caught than taught. First you must see it before you can shape it into reality. From my perspective, vision is the ability to clearly see and articulate where God wants us to go or what He

---
5 Doug Reed, "Holiness Happens," God is a Gift website, Jan 21.

wants us to do. Vision is the bridge between present and future reality. As one man stated, "If you want to find a needle in a haystack it is almost impossible. Yet if you place a magnet on the edge of the haystack, the needles jump out." This metaphor illustrates how vision is that "magnet that attracts followers and resources."[6] I could not have known at that time how the vision God was giving me was a beginning point for the journey I would soon lead for Southern Florida.

Pastors Adalberto and Ninéye Herrera pulled back the curtain of their lives and showed us firsthand how "to ask in faith." They were praying and fasting leaders long before the Cali Church became a praying church. True vision energizes. Prayerless leaders equal prayerless followers. Prayer vision cannot be delegated. People follow what they see. People don't want to be left out. True vision calls, summons, and pulls us forward. It's "the magnet that attracts," Swanson concludes. Prayer leadership brings clarity. People watch their leaders live out what they say they value.

Churches don't become houses of prayer by accident; only by making prayer the heartbeat of church life. Praying churches are comprised of praying people because buildings don't pray. One pastor put prayer back into his Sunday morning service and testified, "It's been transformational." They "slowed their pace a bit" giving ample room to both learn and do prayer together. They stopped talking about prayer and started praying.

> **Prayer Response:** *Father You have promised that those who seek the Lord lack no good thing. Let me lack nothing as I look to You for every need and desire in my life. I pray that You would speak to me personally, so that my vision would align with yours. I pray that You would reveal and confirm the plans you have for me. I thank You that You want to speak to me, and I commit to walking out your vision for my life. Through Jesus Christ, our Lord, Amen.*

---

6 Eric Swanson, "Catching and Casting Vision," Cru, Train & Grow.

Visionary Servant Leadership

God seeks servants, not merely leaders—individuals through whom He can accomplish great things. Servant leaders aim to guide others according to God's plan rather than their own. Unlike traditional roles, servant leadership is not a position one seeks; it is ordained by God. Often, the challenge with Christian leaders lies not in their ignorance of God's will, but in their reluctance to embrace and execute it.

God appoints leaders based on character; the greater the character, the greater the responsibility entrusted to them. The members of Cali Church are called to be fruitful by making disciples who embody the character of Christ. Prayer is the heartbeat of discipleship. Through fasting, praying, and reaching out, they cultivate a community to which God continually adds those who are being saved.

"Intentional discipleship doesn't happen by mistake," writes Laura Atterbury. "It starts small at the personal level, just between you and Jesus. Then it becomes relational between you and another person. Ultimately it goes global to the point that the whole world has a chance to see by your example that Jesus is real."[7] It may be as simple as getting over oneself.

From my visit to Cali, I gained several transformative insights that have reshaped my approach toward living a purposeful, Christ-centered life. I returned with a resolve to adopt a "serve-first mindset," focusing on the needs of others rather than my own. By maintaining a close connection with God—the source of life—I found courage to shift away from self-centeredness, embracing self-denial and a life aimed at serving beyond personal desires.

I learned the importance of tuning in to God's voice and aligning with His vision, which shifts our focus from simply doing to truly being. This change is vital for spiritual growth and realigns our actions with God's deeper purpose.

---

7 Laura Atterbury, "Heartbeat, The Definition of Discipleship," Calvary Baptist Church, November 05, 2014.

Moreover, I realized the power of the Holy Spirit is essential for mirroring the life of Jesus. To live effectively in this manner, we must devote ourselves to serving one Lord, engaging with one Book—the Bible, and nurturing one passion: helping others move one step closer to Jesus. This holistic approach not only deepens one's faith but actively extends it to those around us, fulfilling Christ's command to make disciples.

Prayer Response: *Lord, I confess that the task before me is greater than the strength I possess to achieve it. It seems overwhelming and exhausting. Grant me a fresh infusion of divine strength, and help me not to rely on myself, but on You. In leading let me never fail to follow. In loving let me never fail. When the vision You have given me is realized, may people give glory and honor to You alone. In Jesus' name. Amen.*

Think a Little Bit Bigger

I know vision can be intimidating to you, but the first stage of vision is to think it. Allow God to give you the vision.[8] "*Piensa en grande,*" Pastor Herrera challenged. "Think Big," bigger in fact than we had ever thought before. "Everything starts in the mind." Small thoughts and small thinking chain us. Think like Abraham in Genesis 15:1-6. Pastor Herrera and his staff planted the seed of vision in our minds—seeing things by faith before they happen. Without a clear vision we do not know what to do. We wake up clueless every morning. Without vision we are such small thinkers. "When God gives you the vision, He gives you the support. Vision is easy, not hard. "Ideas are easy. Execution is everything,"[9] says John Doerr. The Holy Spirit sustains the vision. We work together with Him." Synergy happens when servants work for God as His friends and do the things He commands.

The key is to let God give the vision. We must think right if we hope to be right. However courageously you may try to copy another

---
8 Adapted from "Prayer Focus Day 3," The Six Stages of Vision, Jentezen, 28-29.
9 John Doerr, "Measure What Matters," Quotable Quotes, Good Reads.

successful pastor and church's vision, vision cannot be copied; it must be created. It starts with a dream. So, not only think it, but be willing as Pastor Matthew Cork challenged in a sermon series called *"Riskovation,"* to "risk everything to follow God with courageous innovation and intentional pursuit." Vision makes it easier to take that first big step, especially when it looks risky. "Visionary leadership is widely seen as key to strategic change. That's because visionary leadership does not just set the strategic direction—it tells a story about *why* the change is worth pursuing and inspires people to embrace the change."[10] To think that a district with well over sixteen thousand members could be challenged to prayer and fasting was bigger than anything I had ever attempted but I knew it was from God.

> **Prayer Response:** *Father, give me big, holy, audacious, goals that align with your will and plans. If there is any adjustment You would love me to make, don't hesitate to let me know so that I won't waste my time chasing the wind. My prayer for myself, and for others is that together, we can welcome the life of the Holy Spirit in us, changing us from the inside out for His kingdom's sake. May our churches become true houses of prayer for all nations that God can use to turn this world upside down for Jesus Christ. Amen.*[11]

Catch It, Buy It, Seek It!

Vision transcends the mere act of seeing; it is an expansive, deeply profound faculty that goes beyond our physical capabilities. While sight allows us to observe the world as it is, vision invites us to imagine what it could be. It is not just about looking; it's about foreseeing, about crafting a tapestry of possibilities yet to be woven into reality.

Vision is the catalyst for transformation. It fuels our dreams, ignites innovation, and propels us forward toward both personal and collec-

---

10 Nufer Yasin Ates, et al, "Why Visionary Leadership Fails," Harvard Business Review, February 28, 2019.
11 Portions gleaned from Kim Butts, "The Spiritual Challenges and Benefits of True Fasting," Harvest Prayer Ministries, Kim's Blog.

tive metamorphosis. It is the cornerstone of progress, helping us to not only envision a better future but to actively participate in its creation.

Embracing this perspective means cultivating an inner vision that penetrates beyond the apparent, delving into a deeper understanding of our potential and purpose. It challenges us to see not with our eyes, but with our hearts and minds, inspiring us to lead lives marked by growth, impact, and endless possibilities.

1. Catch it. Once you buy-in to the vision, start to get excited about the vision. Getting buy-in is encouraging others to support your vision. I envisioned that each of our churches would become what Jesus said we should be—houses of prayer (*and* fasting). Vision casting is the leader's responsibility. It may require a "change of mentality" but refuse to be "addicted to mediocrity" with no plan, no clue about what you should do. Seek God for a vision forward because "If we keep doing what we've always done we'll get what we always got!" Enrolling others in the vision God has given you is key to gaining buy-in and trust. David Jeremiah concurs, "The only way the corporate Body of Christ will fulfill the mission Christ has given it is for individual Christians to have a vision for fulfilling that mission personally."

2. Buy it. Consider the cost of the vision to determine if you are willing to "pay the price." Paying a price means we allow God to outline the future and willingly cooperate. Changing the function of the church—to win souls for Christ—is not easy. The question is, do we want to stay the way we are or do something big for God? If we do, God will make us effective and fruitful in achieving His purpose and plan. But let's be honest. It will cost us to be a "full-on" visionary leader!

3. Seek it. Don't let anyone talk you out of it. Pursue your God-ordained desires. Pastor Herrera told us that "*The Master's Plan*" was not for lazy Christians. They laid their hands on us and prayed for an "anointing of multiplication," believing that our limitations were in our own minds, not God's. That week alone, 300 people had come to Christ and were beginning the discipleship process. Many of those responded after messages preached by our pastors. We had never seen anything like that before.

> **Prayer Response:** *"Lord, I pray for vision for my life. I pray that you would speak to me personally, so that my vision would align with yours. I pray that you would reveal and confirm the plans you have for me. This is Your promise in Jeremiah 29:11. I thank You that You want to speak to me, and I commit to walking out your vision for my life."*[12] *Amen and Amen.*

4. Get it. Embrace the dream and when you get it, go after it paying the price to see it become a reality. Joel Ryan outlines the process, "God provide(s) the vision. His prophets relay this vision to the people. The people (i.e., us) then have the choice of whether we want to apply it." What you got will show. Show don't tell. Live in such a way that the young will see and be attracted to Jesus. Like the Apostle Paul, when God gives a vision, you must obey it. I would not be a leader who failed to fast and pray. I returned from Cali with dogged determination to fast at least one meal a week. No more excuses.

5. Share it. When God gives you a vision, there is an accompanying compulsion to share it. You must pass it on to others. The first clue that anyone is getting your leadership: Is anyone following? If you pursue your vision; then look over your shoulder and discover no one is following, it is likely you failed to pass the vision on to your congregation. As goes the leader, so goes the followers. Carry yourself with character not charisma. People follow what they see. Let your leadership bring clarity. People watch you live out what you say you value. Consistency builds credibility.

I left Cali praising God for the experience and committed to lead in such a way that God would bless our efforts with Kingdom growth. I did not think I was lazy, but compared to my Colombian brothers and sisters, maybe I was. I knew I didn't want to slip back into old routines

---
12 Adapted from Citizenheights.com, "21 Days of Possible Prayer and Fasting." January 2020.

nor allow my fervor to dissipate. That would be a monumental undertaking given the fact the enemy had launched an all-out attack against one of the largest churches in my Southern Florida District. The thief (Jn.10:10) wants to ruin anything he can get his hands on, even our most God-inspired visions.

> **Prayer Response:** *"Here I am, Lord." Please reveal your vision and goals for me for my heart says yes and Amen to all you have for me. I thank you that you hear my cries and that you know exactly what I need. Father, I thank you for helping me to see again. Help me to see your heart, your plan, and your goodness. Even when I don't understand, help me to praise you beyond what my natural eyes can see. I trust you for every step.[13] 13 Use my life to be a blessing to everyone around me and may the vision You have given me cause others to see your power and blessing. In Jesus' name. Amen.*

Move Out of Inactivity

Many people fail to move out of inactivity because of a lack of vision. With no army, no artillery, and nothing but an animal prod, Shamgar springs into action (Judges 3:31). Once God has given you a vision, it's time for action. When you fast and pray God pays attention. Don't allow yourself to become a demoralized and complacent couch-potato just sitting there. Don't let the enormity of the task keep you from doing what you can. As my pastor father used to tell us boys, "Can't never did anything!" You can't just sit there justifying all the reasons you cannot do what He is asking you to do. "Don't wait for 100 per cent consensus or even majority involvement. Nothing happens until you start. Nothing ever changes by good intentions. Prayer and fasting taps into divine energy that turns our truest intentions into our best efforts. The practice of these spiritual disciplines brings spiritual nutrients to our entire being.

God wants action not excuses. Seek the wrap around Presence of

---

13 Adapted from Victoria Riollano, "A Prayer for Vision," Your Daily Prayer, Crosswalk.com, June 20, 2021.

Almighty God. A lack of decisiveness locks us in insecurity and inactivity. Shamgar knew he couldn't continue down the dead-end road he was on even though the odds against him were six hundred to one. John C. Maxwell tweeted, "Put *behind* you what you *can't* do. Put *before* you what you *can* do." Shamgar exceeded all expectations. Expectations are not the ceiling but the floor. Spirit-anointed leaders do more with less because their weakness becomes an opportunity for God to display His power. Look for a solution rather than make excuses!

God used Shamgar as "an instrument of deliverance." God used him and He will use you. Take the initiative and make the most of your current circumstances to achieve meaningful goals. Focus on what you can do in the present moment, rather than waiting for perfect conditions. By doing your best with the resources and abilities you currently possess, you align yourself with a greater purpose and open pathways to success.

On the flip side, it also serves as a reminder that excuses can become barriers to our progress. If we constantly focus on limitations and reasons why we can't achieve something, we'll likely remain stagnant. By shifting our mindset towards possibilities and solutions, we can overcome obstacles and make significant strides toward our goals.

Prayer Response: *Father in Heaven, thank You for being as patient as You are with us. We recognize that at times fear comes and paralyzes us, keeping us from moving forward even in the things that You desire for us to pursue. We earnestly pray that You will grant us the courage and the boldness to take the first step by faith, knowing that You are with us each step of the way. Help us to speak positively to ourselves based on Your Word about what we can do when we believe You by faith because You know our potential far more than we ever will. Please, help us today to act, we humbly pray, in the name of your dear Son, Amen!*[14]

---

14 Amended from Sherita Thompson, "Stop Making Excuses," They Changed Me, April 3, 2021.

"A Meeting for Clearness"

In *Setting Your Church Free*, Anderson and Mylander warned, "Corporate sins and the shame that goes with them are not limited to Bible times." Again, and again, Jesus commands His churches to repent. No messing around. No delays. No excuses. It is time to change and it's time to change now. Jesus wants quick, decisive action. Many congregations today, possibly including yours, can sometimes engage in sinful behaviors collectively or within significant groups, affecting the spiritual integrity of the community. The way to end the pain and damage is to repent of sinful patterns that we have tolerated. If something seems to be holding you back; if you're not making progress and moving into the Promised Land of God's full blessing; a sacred assembly may be needed. Repentance that leads to a change of direction will get God's people back to normality personally and corporately.

A Sacred Assembly is a good place to announce and renounce; to articulate our sins and renounce our disobedience to God's Word (Joel 1:14). The Friends Church calls such a service a *"Meeting for Clearness."* Solemn assemblies allow for corporate soul-searching and self-examination. Corporate repentance leads to redirection. This could be your moment of grace, a true pivot point when the unclear becomes crystal clear as you discover the truth of your situation. If repentance is the pivot point that turns you and your situation in a whole new direction, what are you waiting for? It's time for "the repenters" to repent. "If your behavior does not change, you have not truly repented, regardless of what you claim." Return to service performed out of love and devotion to Christ (Rev.2:5).[15]

> **Prayer Response:** *Father, I ask by your Holy Spirit to reveal sin and strongholds in my life that are causing my love for You to grow cold and is making me ineffective in Your kingdom. I will cooperate with you as you dismantle and destroy any stronghold that has given the enemy in-*

---
15 Blackaby, Henry; Blackaby, Richard. Flickering Lamps (p. 28). Blackaby Ministries International. Kindle Edition.

fluence over my life. Deliver us from proud thoughts and vain desires, that with reverent and humble hearts we may draw near to You, confessing our faults, confiding in your grace, and finding in You our refuge and strength. In your powerful name. Amen.

Extra Mile Leadership

Coming off the spiritual high of the Cali experience, God prompted me to do something no other leader in my tribe had ever done (to my knowledge) — call for a Solemn Assembly at our District Camp and Conference Center on the shores of beautiful Lake Placid, FL. March 10, 2007, was declared a Day of Prayer and Fasting to humble ourselves before our God and seek Him together hoping for 1,000 fasting respondents. If we had tried to serve God in our own strength and in our own way, we were ready to switch gears and allow the Spirit to move us forward.

I asked the people to come fasting food on that day, but as the leader I felt compelled to ramp it up personally in my spiritual preparation to lead this first ever Day of Prayer and Fasting. If I started fasting four days out, I thought I might be too weak physically. God often calls leaders to do more than they ask their people to do. "Going the extra mile as a leader," expresses Doug Dickerson, "Is what will set you apart from the rest of the pack and will take you farther than you could have without it."[16] Eventually it shows, but no one other than my wife knew my fasting plan, which is as it should be (Matt.6:16). I started three days out. Prayer for me is a running dialogue with God. I felt God would be pleased with a seven meal fast, consuming only liquids. The Lord would be my strength, and He was. How you prepare in private affects how you serve in public. Zig Ziglar famously said, "There are no shortcuts on the extra mile." Leaders who go the extra mile are never content with the status quo or just doing what is acceptable. They possess a compelling desire to excel both personally and professionally.

---

16 Doug Dickerson, "Five Traits of Extra Mile Leaders," Doug Dickerson on Leadership, January 6, 2019.

Prayer Response: *Sovereign Lord, today we choose to put away our love for the world and the things of the world. We will seek first Your Kingdom rule in our hearts and through our lives. We will pursue Your righteousness in our lives, in our families, in our church, and in our world. We know that to follow You in life means that we are also willing to go the extra mile on behalf of others. We can't see beyond today, but You can. We will concern ourselves with today's needs and challenges. Tomorrow belongs to You. In Jesus name. Amen.*[17]

Logic-Defying Obedience

Dianne Neal Matthews wrote, "We may not witness our acts of obedience result in an immediate miracle as Peter did, but it's always the better choice to tell Jesus, '…but because you say so, I will'" (Luke 5:4-6). The phrase, *"…but because you say so I will,"* captures the essence of faith-driven action. It invites us to trust in a higher wisdom, even when circumstances seem unfavorable or when immediate results are not visible. This trust can ultimately lead to transformative experiences and aligns our actions with a purpose beyond our understanding.

Jesus often asks His followers to do something that flies in the face of logic, but faith increases with each step of obedience. We set up two large tents on an open field near the entrance to our camp and rented 800 chairs. Great pressure and resistance had to be overcome just to get to this day—real estate matters, financial pressures, the grind of travel, non-stop superintending. Five days out, doubts appeared on the horizon. I prayed: "Father, am I way off base to call my people to prayer and fasting?" Will the enemy laugh me to scorn?" "Will anybody show up?" Self-doubt is real when an event of this magnitude is undertaken.

Even if what God has directed you to do seems illogical, pray through your doubts. What God requires of you may not be asked

---
[17] "Prayer for Willingness to God the Extra Mile," Partners in Hope, August 6, 2020.

of others. Keep praying until you can say with confidence, "I will not apologize for obeying God. Obedience is never convenient. Fasting calls for self-denial. Some wondered what I was up to. Others called to make excuse for why they were not coming. So, I prayed, *"Honor the obedient as we gather together to obey 2 Chronicles 7:14."* I invited the Holy Spirit to take charge. My faith began to soar, and excitement wasn't far behind, as I thought about what God was going to do.

Is there some logic-defying act of obedience you need to take? The question is dated but relevant: "What would you attempt for God if you knew you would not fail?" Live in such a way that you listen to what the Holy Spirit is saying and doing, and simply follow His leadership. Press on because the blessing is in the obedience not in the logic. As Dr. Daniel Passini blogged in *"Logic Is the Antithesis to Faith*, "Reason ruins our reliance on the Lord, because you may just reason your way right out of obedience."

> **Prayer Response:** *"Lord Jesus, You have proclaimed that if we love You, we will keep Your commandments. Your Word is true. You have revealed to me, Lord, that if I apply the appropriate promises made by you, to situations in my life, your Word works, for it is truth. Grant me a willing heart and the courage to obey You even when I don't understand. Help me to remember, oh loving Father, that my faith relies on believing in your son Jesus Christ and your Word. Not in what I see, reason, or feel."*[18] *Because You say so, I will. In Your holy name. I pray. Amen.*

Unwavering Faith

"Faith is taking the first step even when you don't see the whole staircase." This quote by Martin Luther King, Jr. encapsulates the essence of faith as having the courage to begin a journey or act without

---
18 Cheryce, Rampersad, "Prayer to Walk by Faith Not by Sight," ChristianTT, January 1, 2023.

knowing all the details or outcomes, trusting that the path will unfold as you proceed.

The day before the Solemn Assembly, I had been fasting nearly 36 hours. I tried to get alone to pray, but pressing leadership demands and interruptions were non-stop. Fasting itself is a form of prayer and can be a very effective form of prayer if approached with the right intention, practiced in moderation, and embraced with a humble heart. Fasting made me more spiritually attune. I longed for God to do something in me that could only be attributed to this discipline. Satan barraged with difficulties, disruptions, and doubts, but I submitted myself to God with unwavering faith and persevered. Every time you fast you will get closer to God.

On the Day of Prayer and Fasting, I had fasted six meals and that morning would be seven. I had unusual strength. By faith one-thousand chairs were set up in anticipation that God would draw His people to this holy convocation. I had prayed to the point of relinquishment: "I will accept the number you draw here. One thousand would be a victorious success, gracious Lord, and I will defer all glory to You." Pray. Fast. Prepare like you believe it. Proceed with unwavering faith. Breakthrough is only a fast away. So, take that first step of obedience and trust God to reveal the next step. "You must maintain unwavering faith that you can and will prevail in the end, regardless of the difficulties, and at the same time, have the discipline to confront the most brutal facts of your current reality, whatever they might be."[19]

> **Prayer Response:** *Lord Jesus, give me an unshakable faith. Where I am weak, make me strong. Where I am wavering, help me lay my anchor down. Erase all doubts. Let me demonstrate absolute confidence and believe that*

---
19 James C. Collins, Quote Fancy.

You will grant all my requests, and You will make me live a victorious life on earth. Let your steadfast love cover me and comfort me as I leave the results in your hands. May I find strength knowing You hold me. For in the name of Jesus Christ I pray. Amen.

6

Unlocking the Power of God

C. Peter Wagner once wrote, "God's purpose may be thwarted, or it may be accomplished depending, to one degree or another, on the obedience of His people and their willingness to use the weapons of spiritual warfare that He has provided. God is powerful enough to win any battle, but He has designed things so that the release of His power at a given moment of time often is contingent upon the decisions and the actions of His people."[1] We planned. We fasted. We prayed. We all came hungry and left filled. The District Day of Prayer and Fasting arrived along with nearly six hundred people to seek the face of God together. Best of all God released His power in unforgettable ways as will be further discussed. What happened after the fast ended still amazes me.

> **Prayer Response:** *Father, if Your purpose and plan depends on my obedience, I gladly yield and surrender all my ambitions, hopes, and plans. Your holy will be done in me. Amen.*

---

[1] C. Peter Wagner, quoted by Debbie Przybylski Crosswalk.com, "The Power of Prayer for Supernatural Strength and Authority."

More Than We Ask or Imagine!

The disciplines of fasting and self-control should have a singular focus—to make the followers of Jesus more ready and cheerful to accomplish those things which God would have us do. These practices serve as tools or disciplines that help us prepare ourselves spiritually and mentally. By fostering readiness and cheerfulness, they aim to align our actions and intentions with divine guidance or purpose. Fasting is not just about avoiding food; it is also practiced to develop mental focus, foster humility, and build resilience. Similarly, exercising self-control goes beyond mere restraint; it is an act of mastering oneself, which helps an individual maintain adherence to their personal values and achieve their long-term objectives.

As I fasted, I prayed with expectation that the Holy Spirit would ignite a spark of revival across our district. This is an easy thing for God. Refuse to allow any distraction or resistance to hinder you. Distractions are a ploy of the enemy designed to deter and defeat and have a way of appearing at all the wrong times. Ask for Spirit anointing to face these peripheral tangents. They are the uninvited guests that overshadow our minds to guide us away from the Lord. "But the good news is that we are not hopelessly bound to these invaders. God wants us to know that it is possible to win the battle against the distractions that come at us when we try to pray."[2]

Humbling yourself with fasting brings the inner workings of the Holy Spirit into play in a most unusual and powerful way, especially the ability to stay focused in prayer. There is no greater joy than being in the presence of Jehovah. Invite Him to take charge. Only those accustomed to practicing the presence of Jesus will understand this. Fix your attention on Jesus and allow the Holy Spirit to lift you up, and you will experience God's presence and receive whatever gifts God wants to give to you.

In the wee hours of the morning, I pleaded for the Holy Spirit to descend upon us with great power and effectiveness and we were not

---
[2] The Word Among Us, "Dealing with Distractions in Prayer."

disappointed. Amazing peace attends praying your way into silence and submission. I've learned that I have not prayed well until I have prayed my way to silence in the center of my soul. You need not scream your fears and anxieties away. Simply empty the cargo of your soul and allow Holy Spirit to take charge and receive His anointing. Fasting and prayer fueled by food from above, achieves extraordinary results. Our private encounters with God unleash spiritual power in public. Something deep in me touched something deep in God. Fasting and prayer prepares us for great exploits for Him. Prayer and fasting unleashes the power of God to do exceedingly abundantly above all we ask or think.

Prayer Response: *"Lord, make me so mighty against the deadly undertow of self-reliance that I am never ashamed to trust your arm, like a child with his father, in every breaking wave. Lord, make me so mighty in seeing and mighty in savoring the promises of your sovereign grace that in all my sorrows I might never cease to sing your praise."*[3] *This I pray through Christ my Lord. Amen.*

Unquenchable Fire

When the Spirit draws near with His probing presence, He has the power to pierce through our outward appearances, revealing the concealed aspects of our inner selves and bringing them into the light for reflection and transformation.

Cars and vans loaded with people began rolling through the gate before 9:00 a.m. in anticipation of the 10:00 a.m. starting time. Over 300 people had gathered just prior to starting time. Just then, a caravan of bright yellow school buses with 250 Hispanic people from *Miami Betanía Iglesia* rolled through the gates swelling the crowd to nearly 600. Best of all, the Holy Spirit showed up. Mind-blowing things happen when a gathered group of fasting believers pray in obedience to 2 Chronicles 7:14. It shouldn't surprise us when revival flare-ups break out in places wherever the people of God humble themselves, pray, and seek God's face, and turn from their wicked ways. We are restored

---

3 John Piper, "15 Prayers for God's Power," Desiring God, March 11, 2014.

to spiritual health when we allow God to the deal with the things that are defeating or detracting us and hindering our prayers from being answered.

Rather than recite a litany of corporate repentance, each person was given a blank 3 X 5 card and asked to write down any wicked way (sin) the Spirit might reveal; then bring it to one of the chimeneas at the corners of the tent. Just then, a morning dove flew into the tent and landed upon the lectern. It seemed so symbolic. The Holy Spirit descended as cards were cast into the consuming flames as a visual reminder of how God removes our sins from us as we name them and repent. Cleansing ourselves of sin gives the Holy Spirit the opportunity to write on our card our greatest hindrances to prayer; then opens the door to Jesus to let him minister to us in our need.

The Spirit had prompted the idea. Only He could have orchestrated the response. Hundreds of people, young and old, hunched over their open Bibles writing down hindrances they wanted to be rid of. One-by-one they stood to their feet and streamed forward to surrender their sins or shortcomings to the flame. Nearly everyone came forward as the Spirit suggested displeasing things from which they needed to turn away. The Holy Spirit brings conviction of sin for the purpose of repentance. Repentance puts us on praying ground because iniquity has not been disregarded (Ps.66:18). Christians are also called by Scripture to maintain repentant hearts by routinely acknowledging sin and seeking God's grace and mercy in the face of our daily missteps that need God's forgiving grace. True revival is characterized by a spirit of repentance.

Prayer Response: *Lord, you are indeed a consuming fire (Heb. 12:29)! Come Holy Spirit, fill the hearts of Your faithful and rekindle in us the fire of your love. Come upon our Church in abundance and overwhelm the chaff of sin and confusion that has crept its way onto our hearth. Clear away any chaff or debris within us. Do a deep and lasting work of transformation from the inside* *out. Set my heart ablaze with Your glory so I can obey what You ask me to do and reveal Your nature and power to others through my life. In Jesus' name. Amen.*

"Prayer in Motion"

The Spirit's call to "Go and walk through the land" highlights the importance of active participation in realizing our potential and embracing divine promises (Genesis 13:17). While prayer and reflection play crucial roles, they need to be paired with decisive action to be effective. Simply waiting and complaining will not create change. Instead, we must take informed and purposeful steps to progress toward our goals and realize the promises that await us. Rick Shepherd calls "Prayer walking, prayer in motion or prayer on location."[4]

We gathered. We repented of any sin in our hearts the Spirit revealed. Then we stood together in the presence of a Holy God with clean hands and pure hearts. We didn't remove our shoes, but everyone knew we were standing on holy ground. Repentance clears the path to intercession (Ps.66:18). The Spirit had prompted us to pray the whole Bible over our 93-acres of Florida sand. Like Abraham, the people were sent on a prayer walk of the entire campus reading and praying every chapter and verse over the land in every direction. If they did not have a Scripture to read, we asked them to prayer walk hosting the Presence and power of God on our campus.

The people prayed through one passage or verse covering our campground in intercessory prayer at the direction of the Holy Spirit. There are far-reaching though unforeseeable benefits to entertaining God at your home, your church, or even your business. There is no greater privilege than being a host to God Himself. He went looking for people who would host His Presence and found them in a South-Central Florida town called Lake Placid. An hour later, having completed the reading each of the Bible's 31,102 verses, we returned to the tent for a closing time of intercessory prayer. That day a parcel of the Southern

---
[4] Rick Shepherd, "Prayer Walking, Prayer in Motion," Prayer and Spiritual Awakening Department, Florida Baptist Convention.

Florida landscape turned into holy ground.

Barrenness was broken and fruitfulness followed as will be seen. Ever since, that real estate has had a compelling anointing. Most spiritually attune visitors can sense it the moment they drive through the gates. Holy things happen there. Hundreds, if not thousands, have been saved, filled with the Holy Spirit and called into Christian service since that glorious Spring Day. If you have never taken a prayer walk start in your own neighborhood. Pray for each house on your block or prayer walk your church property. Missionary Harmon Schmelzenbach prayer walked a piece of land in Nairobi, Kenya. The thriving university the Nazarenes have there today is testimony to that prayer walk Harmon took. God gave the Church of the Nazarene every inch of the ground he encircled!

Prayer Response: *Lord Jesus, I pray for my neighbors [insert names] that they'll come to full understanding of their sin and come to know your amazing grace and salvation. Wrap them in your love and help me to shine your love to them as well. Bless them as they seek You and protect them from anyone or anything that will hinder their walk with You. In Jesus' name. Amen.*

The Amazing Exchange

Isaiah 58:11b paints a picture of spiritual abundance and vitality, likening faithful individuals to a well-watered garden and an ever-flowing spring. This passage underscores the rejuvenating effect of divine connection. Mahesh Chavda emphasizes that fasting is not a transactional act to gain favor, but a spiritual discipline aimed at strengthening our connection with God. By fasting, we clear away the distractions and blockages that cloud our spiritual "pipeline," allowing the divine anointing and sustenance to flow more freely into our lives, enhancing our spiritual health and growth.

Fruitfulness is one of the amazing results of acceptable fasting that Isaiah lists. We can expect God's blessing to result in more disciples made and his gracious provision in our lives. God will use some of us to be rebuilders and restorers of walls (Isa. 58:12). Acceptable fasting turns wastelands into fruitful groves, "graveyards into gardens." God wants to turn our churches and communities from wastelands to well-watered gardens or groves where spiritual fruit is growing! What an amazing exchange: dry arid wastelands for well-watered gardens! You probably wouldn't be shocked to realize that if we, our churches, and our ministries are not bearing fruit (making disciples), we're subject to pruning and the fire (Jn.15:6). Don't miss the bottom line: If we do not bear fruit, we are displeasing to God which was never His intention for us.

Christian brothers and sisters from all denominations heard about this holy place. The ministry experienced growth and blessing beyond anything we could imagine or think. Income quadrupled. Over 60,000 patrons now visit annually. A million-dollar estate gift was received. Visitors are saved. Young people are called to full-time Christian service. Marriages are healed and restored. Signs and wonders have been reported. All, the result a two-hour event that God turned into an unforgettable four-hour Prayer meeting!

The skeptical who wondered whether it would be worth the time and effort left convinced of the power of prayer and fasting. The Holy Spirit did the preaching. God changed hearts and minds. We left on a spiritual high. We had been to the mountain and God had come down, filling us with joy and the unspeakable glory of His holy Presence. It was a summit moment. Everyone paused to ponder the beauty of what just happened, and just take it all in.

> **Prayer Response:** *Lord Jesus, I pray that I might not only bear fruit, but much fruit for Your glory. May I not be a branch that is barren, a branch that is "thrown into the fire" (Jn.15:6). And now I pray for [insert name(s)] that they might come to know You and trust You*

with their lives and future. I pray that they might see that they cannot change themselves; You do not expect us to bear fruit by our will power but by dependence on You and Your blessed Spirit. In your name. Amen.[5]

Signs and Wonders

Hebrews 2:4 speaks to the ways in which God has confirmed His message and presence through signs, wonders, miracles, and the gifts of the Holy Spirit. These divine acts serve as evidence of His power and involvement in the world. C Joybell C suggests a shift in focus from seeking external signs to cultivating internal spiritual sight. Rather than asking for miraculous signs as proof, we should seek the vision and discernment to perceive God's work and presence in our lives and the world around us. This internal sight enables deeper understanding and awareness of divine guidance and truth.

Jeff Keaton in his book, *Radical Faith* states, "When we're willing to live by radical faith, God will give us the strength to obey Him, and miraculous signs will follow." In June 2007, a group from the *El Rey Jesus* church in Miami, had gathered to worship on the lakeside beach in front of the stationary cross. Suddenly, a cloud rose on the far side of the lake. There were no other clouds in the sky. Suddenly, a face appeared in the clouds with lightning from the top of his head to the lake. No one would ever convince the worshipers that day that it was none other than the face of Jesus! And He was smiling. Somebody captured the miraculous sign with their camera video. And then the cloud disappeared.

Seth Troutt explains, "Signs and wonders are different ways of talking about miracles. Signs point beyond themselves to a greater meaning, concept, or purpose." Further, he clarifies, "A sign appeals to the understanding, a wonder appeals to the imagination. 'Signs' emphasize *what* the miracle proves, and 'wonder' emphasizes *how* the miracle inspires worship."[6] Such supernatural manifestations do not occur of-

---

5 Dr. Erwin W. Lutzer, "A Prayer for Fruitfulness," Moody Church Media, February 24, 2013.
6 Seth Troutt, "How Should We Be Thinking About Signs and Wonders Today?" Redemption Gateway, February 24, 2023.

ten, but the Hebrew writer affirms that God testifies with them according to His own will. Signs are not what "fundamentally supernatural people" seek after. We seek Him. They point to a greater reality—the One who saves. God doesn't have to knock our socks off every time we gather to worship, but we should expect His presence and power often and repeatedly. Miracles of grace occur with every transformed life (2 Cor.5:17). When we seek God's face in prayer and fasting and worship, He sometimes shows up in earth shattering ways (Acts 4:31). If you think miracles were confined to biblical times or that anything that happens can be explained scientifically, it leads to cynicism. But time and again God proves otherwise. I still believe that God sovereignly works miracles without the agency of any human being and in answer to our prayers. Sam Storms said, "Miracles are to be prayed for. The spiritual gift of working miracles is one that we should all seek. Whether or not it is given is entirely up to God."[7]

> **Prayer Response:** *Father, I ask You to fill and embolden us to proclaim the living Christ. Please show up in our cities again. Show up in our lives with signs and wonders designed to demonstrate to believers and unbelievers that you are alive. Start with me. [Name the miracle you need]. In Jesus' name. Amen.*

The Secret Benefits of Fasting

Perhaps our reluctance to fast stems from a focus on the deprivation aspect—what we are giving up—rather than the spiritual benefits we gain. By changing our view of fasting to see it as a tool for deeper spiritual connection, insight, and renewal, we can embrace it as a revitalizing practice that infuses us with the power of the Spirit. This mirrors the transformative experience of the prophet in Micah 3:8, where such spiritual practices lead to profound empowerment. This focus on the positive spiritual outcomes can encourage more frequent and meaningful engagement with fasting.

---
[7] Sam Storms, "#59 Are Signs, Wonders, and Miracles For Today?: Romans 15:18-19," June 12, 2022.

Spiritual benefits aside, amazing physical strength and stamina seem to accompany fasting. Prayer and fasting enable you to glide in the Jetstream of the Spirit infusing you with extraordinary strength and stamina. Prior to the Solemn Assembly, I had not eaten since the previous Wednesday night and would not break my fast until after 4:00 p.m. Fasting deepened my dependence upon the Lord for strength. There was no time to rest. I was scheduled to preach three times the next day. On top of that, we turned our clocks forward for Daylight Savings Time losing an hour's sleep. Awake at 5:00 a.m. with an hour-and-a-half drive ahead of me, I asked the Father to show me what to preach. Feeling the effects of that loss of an hour's sleep, the Spirit drew me to David's prayer: *"… Grant your strength to your servant."* (Ps. 86:16, NASB). Then to God's promise to Moses, *"… Your strength will equal your days."* (Deut. 33:25, NIV). We arrived at our first stop with a half-hour to spare.

Perhaps not surprisingly, by the time we arrived, the Spirit had directed me to Mark 9 where the disciples' exorcism had failed. They asked Him, "Why?" *"This kind can only be cast out by prayer (and fasting),"* Jesus replied. Incredible anointing to preach with passion and freedom without notes complemented the anointing. Fasting unlocks the power of prayer with amazing results. That afternoon we traveled south to preach yet again. I called for prayer partners in both places and another 100 intercessors responded. I arrived home just before midnight. My strength had been renewed. I had soared on eagle's wings. I had run hard without weariness and walked without fainting. There's more.

Prayer Response: *Lord, I thank You for the many times You have given me the endurance to keep going, even when things are tough. Please bless me with your strength and peace. Your Word says the joy of the Lord is my strength. If that's true, then I ask for a fresh infusion of your joy to replace all the bone-tired parts of my mind, body, and soul. You know the times I have been near the point of exhaustion doing the work You have given me to* *do. I throw off the spirit of heaviness and exchange it for a garment of praise. Thank You for the superhuman energy which You so mightily enkindle and work within me. In the name of Jesus I pray, Amen.*[8]

Strength for the Journey

Prayer and fasting prepare us for the epic tasks before us in a way no other spiritual regimen can. You will literally travel from strength to strength (Psalm 84:7) and have more power than you ever dreamed. Fresh off the Day of Prayer and Fasting having preached three times and traveled over 400 miles, I drove to Miami the next day for a flight to Nashville, TN, to fulfill my responsibility on the Board of Trustees at my Alma Mater, Trevecca Nazarene University. Because of time constraints, I absconded from the closing session of the board meeting to fly to Washington-Dulles enroute to Brussels. Our departure was delayed four hours by a late Spring Nor'easter blanketing the planes and runways with snow and ice. My destination: Kigali, Rwanda, for a Leadership Training Conference with thirty-four handpicked leaders from across the French Equatorial District of Africa. I made the connecting flight in Brussels, but my luggage did not. So, I arrived in Kigali prepared to stay at the mission compound but there was no water or electricity. I did not protest too loudly when asked to stay in the Alpha Palace Hotel the entire week though I had only the clothes I was wearing.

The farther you travel, instead of being faint and weary, as travelers in such cases are wont to be, the stronger you grow. He refreshes us with each twist and turn and demand of our journey. Far from depleting energy and strength, fasting allows God to intervene and move you forward. Fasting is not just for super Christians but for Christians in desperate need of supernatural strength. Make it part of your everyday life and watch mountains move because of your deeper connection with God. Invite God into your burdens; draw close to Him and you will finish strong, no matter what age or circumstance. Looking back,

---
8 Portions gleaned from Prayers that Avail Much, "To Overcome Fatigue."

the spiritual and physical benefits that followed my fasting are mind-blowing. The little I sacrificed to God, the more His gift to me. In the words of Michelle Eagle, fasting "is His way of focusing me, pulling me close. When I was hungry for food, I needed to be reminded to be hungry for God. This insight helped change my fasts into an act of worship, a time of praise."9 I learned to "lean into God in a surrendered, steadfast prayer," and "feasting upon God" gave strength beyond compare.

> **Prayer Response:** *Lord, grant me grace and strength equal to the demands before me. Your strength keeps me running the race faithfully, as I find strength in that safe, secret place under the shadow of the Almighty. My weakness and weariness are infused with strength and power because I rely not on myself but on You. You never intended for me to hang on to my own strength or use it to get Your work done. Thank you for the freedom and peace You give to those walking close to You. Amen.*

Anointing to Preach

Where does the anointing we seek originate? This divine anointing equips and empowers us to execute God's mission, spreading hope and transformation far and wide. God's anointing surpasses earthly limitations—it is not confined to any position or portfolio. This divine empowerment is accessible to everyone, irrespective of their social status, enabling everyone to pursue their unique calling with God-given authority and purpose. The potential is limitless for those touched by the Spirit.

I had traveled over 8,300 nautical miles to get to Kigali. My Bible and notes were in Brussels but preach I must at a New Start congregation in Nyamirambo. I borrowed a Bible from my host and the Spirit drew me to Romans 8:28-39 praying all the while that God would come through once again for His travel-weary servant. As we worshipped the Spirit came down in the dimly lit room, a shaft of sunlight

---

9 Michelle Eagle, "Fasting: A Surprising Journey into Joy," Renew.org.

piercing through one small window. I settled on those words, *"If God is for us, who can be against us"* (Rom. 8:31)? Satan, the thief, condemns, thwarts, and seeks to separate and isolate us from God's love. Regardless of what may come against us, nor the accusations Satan fires against us, we are secure in God's love. I reminded us all who God is and how He helps us. When we grasp the truth that God is for us, we have nothing to fear. He is on our side; He is working on our behalf and for our good. He has proved His benevolence in that He has adopted us (Rom.8:15), He has given us His Spirit (verses 16–17, 26–27), and He has determined to save us (verses 29–30).

Pastor Moise gave an impassioned invitation, and one lone man gave his heart to Christ, a fresh miracle of grace. Ten others stood in response to the invitation. The anointing to preach good news "knows no limits" or location. This anointing is for everyone regardless of the size of the assignment. God will anoint you with power and strength for whatever He has asked you to do. Spirit anointing is but one of the secret benefits of prayer and fasting. Prayer and fasting invites an anointing that provides a fresh demonstration to a watching world that Jesus is not dead He is alive. Billy Graham once said, "When we rely on the Holy Spirit, He sanctifies and empowers us so we can be effective tools in God's hands." Forget not all His benefits. "Programs, propaganda, pep, and personality are not enough," charged Vance Havner. "There must be power. God's work must be done by God's people God's way."

> **Prayer Response:** *Lord Jesus, You are my rock, and I run to you today, believing that you will lift my heavy arms, that you will fuel me for the tasks you've given me, and that your joy will completely consume the weakness of my life and make me strong again. I know that because of You I am ultimately a victor when my reservoir of strength is depleted. I know that nothing in this world can separate me from your steadfast love. Please give me a measure of your love today; give me the strength to endure this day's demands. In your powerful name. Amen.*[10]

---

10 Adapted from Rebecca Barlow Jordan, "Prayers for Strength to Find Comfort and Hope," Crosswalk.com, March 7, 2022

The Anointing of Multiplication

Transformative power is available to believers, empowering us to continue Christ's work and make even greater impact through faith (John 14:12). Central to the Kingdom of God is the multiplication and growth of Christian churches, a vital part of extending Christ's mission on earth. Prayer serves as the chief instrument through which believers can release God's purposes into reality, enabling the flourishing of His kingdom. Together, faith in Jesus and the power of prayer catalyze the expansion and vitality of the church, fulfilling God's divine intentions.

Prayer and fasting prepare the way for God to give us a fresh vision and a crystal-clear purpose. "We cannot be indifferent to prayer (nor fasting)," Pastor Herrera had told us. "A body indifferent to breathing is dead. It does not care; it is no longer alive. Its lamp does not burn. In addition, he had prayed for an *"anointing of multiplication."* His prayer began to be answered through "leadership multiplication"—leaders reproducing leaders. Adalberto had modeled spending more time with less people to achieve greater results. Jesus invested himself in twelve men one of whom would betray him. I invested a week in the lives of 34 leaders who in turn would train at least 500 other African pastors.

Things I learned in Cali, I began to understand about prayer and fasting. Pastor Herrera awakens at 4:00 a.m. every day and personally participates, in at least four prayer meetings each week. People follow what they see. "A leader knows the way, goes the way, and shows the way" (Maxwell). The Cali Church has five two-hour services every Sunday to accommodate the crowds, and Adalberto preaches all of them. Where does the strength and anointing to passionately preach five times come from? (I've been told that one message vigorously preached is the equivalent of eight hours of work). Only by prayer and fasting. These "therapeutic regimens" also give wisdom to delegate and develop leaders, thus allowing "the fruit of his ministry to grow on other people's trees."

Prayer Response: *Father I pray [insert your pastor/spiritual leaders] may not be distracted, discouraged or doubtful and thus neglect the spiritual gift You have given him/her. Give them the tenacity to take great pains to maintain the path You have cleared for them and to be absorbed in the work You have laid before them" (1 Tim. 4:14-15). Lord, I pray that You would send a spirit of encouragement to [insert name(s)] so that they might walk in a manner of the calling with which they have been called; lead them to walk with all humility and gentleness, with patience, showing tolerance for those around them in love, and that they would be diligent to preserve the unity of the Spirit in the bond of peace (Eph.4:1-3).*[11]

"Therapeutic Regimens"

Fasting, as an expression of humility, underscores the spiritual discipline of self-denial to forge a deeper connection with God, as highlighted in Psalm 35:13. Together with prayer, fasting forms what can be seen as 'therapeutic regimens'—practices that align the spirit and body towards divine purposes. These regimens yield powerful results, as they open the heart to transformation, clarity, and strength. Through prayer and fasting, believers cultivate a space for God's presence, guidance, and healing, allowing them to experience profound spiritual growth and empowerment.

Prayer and fasting are often linked together in Scripture with powerful results. Simply to go without food is at best a good physical discipline. Praying rather than eating reaps powerful results! Prayer encounters God. Fasting confronts the flesh-dominated self. Consider the benefits of refraining from eating or drinking for a period as an act of worship that is good for your soul:

Fasting is the biblical way to humble yourself in sight of God. "The discipline of fasting will humble you, remind you of your dependency

---
11 Gleaned from April Motl, "10 Powerful Prayers for Pastors and Leaders," Crosswalk.com, June 28. 2019.

on God, and bring you back to your first love. Many have allowed fasting to become "a neglected discipline." Ought we to at least consider "the spiritual possibilities" latent in fasting? "When we detox the spirit and become consumed with desire and praise for God, we become sensitive to His voice."[12]

1. Fasting reveals our true spiritual condition, often resulting in brokenness, repentance, and change. The Holy Spirit often uses our fast to reveal some hidden sins displeasing to God and preventing His blessing. It allows us to confront the sin and pray for power to live a holy, sanctified life. Simply put, we need this "soul cleansing." It is a "strong faith-move," filled with expectation that God will fill us afresh with His Holy Spirit.

2. Fasting is a crucial means for dynamic personal revival. Do you seek renewal in your spiritual life? Consider fasting. It renews and will break you out of the world's routine. Your relationship with Jesus is bound to go deeper. God may even use you to be a channel of revival in your church. "God, the sustainer of all life, wants nothing more than a closer connection with us, and through the spiritual benefits of fasting we can quench that new desire for more of Him in our lives."[13]

> **Prayer Response:** *"God, You are my God, and I seek You earnestly (Ps. 63:1). I seek You as I undertake this fast. I bow before You and ask You to purge me of all unworthy thoughts, words, and deeds. Forgive my sins as I forgive those who have sinned against me. Keep me strong and alert during my fast. Protect me from the Evil One, deliver me from temptation and steer my mind and heart away from all distractions. Help me to bring my spirit, soul, body, and mind into subjection and focus them on You, to Whom all praise belongs, Amen."*[14]

---

12 Brooke Obie, "5 Spiritual Benefits of Fasting," Guideposts.
13 Ibid.
14 The Editors, "10 Inspiring Prayers for Lent and Fasting," Guideposts.

"The Three-ply Cord"

Ecclesiastes 4:12 in the Common English Bible teaches us about the strength found in unity: *"Also, one can be overpowered, but two together can put up resistance. A three-ply cord doesn't easily snap."* Combined efforts significantly enhance resilience and effectiveness. When considering individual discipline, fasting emerges as the single most effective answer to over-nourishment, offering a pathway to balance and spiritual strength. Just as community and solidarity provide a united front, integrating fasting with other spiritual practices like prayer creates a fortified approach to personal growth and self-control. This holistic combination strengthens individuals much like a three-ply cord, making them less susceptible to the difficulties posed by physical and spiritual challenges.

In Matthew 6, Jesus taught three duties of every Christian—giving, praying, and fasting—vital principles that often conflict with the those of prevailing culture. All three practices should be a normal part of the Christian life. We should pay as much attention to fasting as we give to praying and giving. When each cord of discipline is braided together in your life and a community of faith, it will not easily snap or be broken when the stresses of life and ministry press in on us. They make us as strong as a triple braided cord.

Do you excel in the grace of giving? Do you struggle with money, especially the concept of tithing? Give the first 10 percent of your earnings to God if for no other reason than to dethrone greed from your heart. Don't focus on the percentage you give; rather on what you keep. Let your giving flow from the gratitude of a converted heart.

Do you practice the discipline of prayer? Or do you just pay lip service to prayer without doing much praying? If you think you are too busy to pray, you're too busy! If you don't pray, you're saying to God that you can handle life and its challenges all by yourself. You can't, and I know it's humbling to admit, without Christ we can do nothing.

Do you practice the discipline of fasting? Hungry people are desperate people. Every time you fast to pray you will get closer to God (Matt.5:6). You might even see Him do the impossible! Combine these three disciplines and see what God will do! When these disciplines are done with right motives, God delights in meeting our needs.

> **Prayer Response:** *Lord Jesus, I give up myself, my life, my all, utterly to You, to be yours forever. I hand over to your keeping all my friendships; all the people whom I love are to take second place in my heart. Fill me now and seal me with Your Spirit. Work out your whole will in my life at any cost, for to me to live is Christ. Move my heart toward a greater trust in You. I surrender my will to Your will. I swing wide the door for You to work in me and through me in ways I never imagined before. Amen.*[15]

Pursue a Fasted Lifestyle

Ezra 8:22b-23 in the Common English Bible highlights the connection between seeking divine guidance and experiencing God's favor: *"The power of God favors all who seek him… So, we fasted and prayed to our God for this, and he responded to us."* This passage illustrates the potent combination of fasting and prayer as a means to receive God's response and intervention.

Dave Williams, in *The Miracle Results of Fasting*, echoes this sentiment, noting that we are living in a remarkable period where God is calling people to fast. By engaging in this discipline, believers are drawn closer to God, empowering them to win souls, exercise spiritual authority, and advance His kingdom. Fasting, when practiced with sincere purpose, becomes a transformative journey that not only deepens personal faith but also extends God's impact through their lives, resonating with the call to be active participants in His divine plans.

---

15 Adapted from Sarah Doss, "Spiritual Disciplines | Prayer," Lifeway.women, October 4, 2018.

Those who pray pursue a lifestyle of fasting because Satan hates it. Jesus' victory over satan's mighty onslaught of temptation came because of fasting (Lk.4). Pursue the fast that God has chosen but expect the rewards to come *after* not *during* a fast.

In the pages to follow I will describe the powerful results that always accompany prayer and fasting. You will discover how fasting releases the anointing of the Spirit in a way I cannot fully explain. It affects the work of God in the lives of His people and His church. I discovered this truth about living a fasted life: "it will keep you on miracle territory every day."

Fasting is a great way to begin a New Year. For seven consecutive years, I encouraged my people on the Southern Florida District to join me in a 21-day Daniel Fast with a specific focus for our fasting. It is not only a great way to begin the year, but it also sets the course for the rest of the year. Many pastors and churches continue this discipline to this day. Start fasting. Begin small but challenge yourself physically and spiritually to a deeper level of seeking God. Philip Renner says of the fasted life, "It's not about sacrificing food but a lifestyle of quieting the flesh to say yes to the voice of God."[16] Pursue a fasted lifestyle, and you will begin to see an enormous difference in the miracle terrain. I know I did.

Prayer Response: *Dear Heavenly Father, thank You for hearing and answering my prayer, Abba Father. Please help me remember to continue praying and fasting for Your anointing. And I pray that You would do such a work in my heart that Your power and anointing are similarly able to flow in my life without measure. I am desperate for You. Thank You for touching me with Your anointing and power right now. Holy Spirit rest on me enabling me to do whatever You need me to do. In Jesus' holy and precious name. I pray, Amen.*[17]

---

16 Philip Renner, A Fasted Life: Living a Lifestyle of Intimacy and Power with God, (Shippensburg: Harrison House Publishers, 2021) promo keynote.
17 Adapted from His Presence, "Prayer for More Anointing."

Spiritual Blessings Flow Through Fasting

Rich spiritual blessings are available to those who are in Christ Jesus (Eph.1:3). The discipline of fasting aligns with this promise by serving as a powerful spiritual practice that can open the believer to these blessings. It is often said that fasting releases the anointing, the favor, and the blessing of God in the life of a Christian. Through fasting, believers intentionally make space for God's presence, allowing them to more fully receive and recognize the spiritual blessings that are already theirs in Christ. By dedicating time and focus to God, fasting amplifies spiritual awareness and creates a deeper connection to the divine, enabling Christians to experience God's favor and anointing in new and impactful ways.

Three other spiritual blessings are released by fasting:

1. Fasting helps us better understand God's Word by making it more meaningful, vital, and practical. He uses the Word to bless us and bolster us when the load gets heavy. After I preached in the 11:00 a.m. service in Cali, a woman came up to me and handed me a note she had scribbled in Spanish. She thanked the Lord for my life, because in it, what He says in Deuteronomy 33:25, KJV is true: *"And as thy days, so shall thy strength be."*

2. Fasting causes us to be more spiritually attentive. It quiets our inner self so we can focus on God and helps us gain power over physical desires. Fasting puts us in sync with Holy Spirit, our Source of power. Fasting is great preparation for the spirit, soul and body when you face a formidable task. Do you long for amazing things in your life? "Don't just say you will fast when God lays it on you or you never will," D.L. Moody cautioned, "We are too cold and indifferent. Take the yoke upon you."

3. Fasting transforms prayer into a richer and more intimate experience. Again, fasting puts us in touch with the Holy Spirit allowing Him to breathe in us. It is almost impossible to be a disinterested worshiper when you are fasting. "Abstinence from food," William Mac-

Donald would say, "can be a valuable aid in spiritual exercises." So put prayer before necessary food and see what God will do.

Other benefits we dare not miss include power to overcome satanic influence, preparation to meet life's challenges and pressures, not to mention Spirit articulation of God's will and plan. Fasting anticipates God's intervention and deliverance and helps us grow in gratitude when He does. Need strength to hard things? "Fasting is a discipline that teaches us to trust in God for our strength."[18]

> **Prayer Response:** *Enable me to hear Your still small voice. Grant me a fresh vision of your call and purpose for my life. Remove all confusion. Speak to me and guide me as I fast. Your Word is true, and it abides forever. It will not return to You void. You are faithful and just and true and righteous, and You are my Source, my Strength, and my Provider. I ask You to do what You have promised me in Your Word that You would do. Change me and work miracles on my behalf I pray in Jesus' name. Amen.*[19]

"Consecrate a Fast"

Abundant spiritual blessings are accessible to those who are united with Christ (Eph.1:3). Fasting as a spiritual discipline can facilitate a deeper reception and awareness of these blessings. It is often viewed as a practice that releases God's anointing, favor, and blessing into the life of a Christian. By choosing to fast, believers create intentional space in their hearts and minds for God's presence, enabling them to better perceive and experience the spiritual blessings they have in Christ. Fasting heightens spiritual sensitivity and fosters a closer relationship with God, empowering Christians to experience His favor and anointing more fully and profoundly. God may call you to *"consecrate a fast"* at any time convenient or not. If you work in an office in proximity with associates and friends, it is difficult to hide the fact that you are not going to lunch or snacking at your desk. When five-year-old Abbey, with the help of her mother, stopped by my office with a plate of just-baked

---
18 Ascension, "Spiritual Benefits of Fasting."
19 Adapted from Jamie Rohrbaugh, "A Prayer for Unction to Fast and Pray."

gooey, chocolate chip cookies, I thanked them but set them aside for later consumption when my fasting had ended. When you're fasting, it's not a good time to sit in front of the TV and watch those enticing pizza commercials with stretchy, gooey cheese oozing through the flat screen! There is no convenient time to consecrate a fast, so just do it! Simply set aside a time to forget about food and to seek God.

Every time you fast you establish a new spiritual dimension in your life. You'll be amazed at the spiritual benefits to say nothing about the health benefits of fasting. During a 21-day Daniel Fast I typically lost twelve lbs. I can't guarantee that for you but there is documented scientific evidence that fasting benefits health.[20] The Early Church fasted on Wednesdays or Fridays because the Scribes and Pharisees fasted on Tuesdays and Thursdays, and they did not want to be confused with those who fasted to be seen of men. Fasting for show didn't impress Jesus then; it will not impress Him now. Fasting is obedience, nothing else! When we add fasting to our prayers, God's power is released to say nothing of the affront to satan as we have noted. Fasting should always be a normal part of a relationship with God. It has incredible power to unclutter our spirit from the things of this world and make us amazingly sensitive to the things of God.

> **Prayer Response:** *Lord, my eyes are opening to the benefits of fasting. Now, I open my heart to you like never before. Give me unction to pray and fast and turn to You with my whole heart, with all my soul, and with all my strength. May I no longer live by bread alone but by every word that comes from your mouth, oh Lord. Teach me to fast so that I might hold fast to you. And as I fast, would you manifest all the answers to the prayers I prayed during my fast? Guide me further on my fasting journey and help me to remain resilient, strengthened in Faith and Scripture. In Jesus' name. Amen.*

---

20 Healthline, "8 Health Benefits of Fasting, Backed by Science," March 13, 2023.

7

Fasting Rocks Your World!

"If we don't fast, we will never know what God could or would have done. Fasting is how you exercise your 'no' muscle. Spiritually speaking, nothing will take your further, faster than fasting. We must fast unto God, but it breaks strongholds and yields breakthroughs."[1]

–Mark Batterson

For the pragmatists reading this, one of your first questions may be whether fasting does any good. The spiritual benefits of fasting have already been highlighted. You will draw closer to God as your soul gets in tune with God's Spirit. Fasting also rocks the body. There is more, and that includes physical well-being and health. The good news is that there are numerous types of fasts. All biblical fasts involve abstaining from some or all food, drink, or both, for a period. Three categories I will highlight here:

1. The ***normal fast*** in which you do not eat any solid food, consuming only clear liquids, such as fruit juices and clear soups (broths).

---
[1] Mark Batterson, If (Grand Rapids: Baker Book House, 2015) 48.

2. The ***absolute fast*** is no food or water at all. Incidentally, only two people on record did such a thing: Moses and Jesus. It is not recommended! "With no food and no water, the maximum time the body can survive is thought to be about one week. With water only, but no food, survival time may extend up to 2 to 3 months."[2]

3. The ***partial fast*** omits certain foods from your diet and/or limit your meals.

How long should you fast? One meal, one day; sunrise to sunset; one day; 24 hours; one week/7 days; 21 days; 30 days; or 40 days. "However long you fast, expect challenges and plan for how to overcome the challenges."[3]

> **Prayer Response:** *Father, I ask You to fill my heart with the peace and joy that comes from trusting that your grace and mercy are enough for me. I pray that the Holy Spirit would guide me in the challenge to lead the fasted life. This is new to me, Lord, and I still have many questions. Draw me closer to You and satisfy the longings of my soul today. In Jesus' name, Amen.*

Give Your Body a Break!

Psalm 138:3 in the New Living Translation expresses the immediate response and encouragement that comes from God through prayer (and fasting): *"As soon as I pray, you answer me; you encourage me by giving me strength."* This verse captures the intimate relationship between seeking God and receiving His strength and support.

Rex Russell, M.D.'s suggestion that our bodies were designed for periodic rests from food, aligns with the idea that fasting is a natural and beneficial practice. From a spiritual perspective, fasting can enhance one's connection with God. By taking a break from physical sustenance, believers can focus more on spiritual nourishment and seek God's presence more earnestly. The combination of prayer and fasting

---
[2] Natalie Silver, "How Long Can You Survive Without Food?" Healthline, January 19, 2024.
[3] Hike to Eternity, "Rock Your Body." Powerfulfasting.com.

can lead to greater spiritual clarity, strength, and encouragement, aligning with the biblical theme of God's prompt response to those who seek Him.

Amazing things happen physically and spiritually. Dr. Russell calls fasting "giving our bodies a break," because just as "the seventh day was designed for rest; the digestive system needs rest just as much as the rest of the body."[4] "It is not wrong to fast," reminds Warren W. Wiersbe, "if we do it in the right way and with the right motive." Consider these benefits:

1. Fasting increased my physical stamina infusing my body with strength to withstand an overstuffed schedule.

2. Fasting heightened my spiritual awareness. I felt like I was on such intimate terms with my Lord that as soon as I prayed, the Lord would answer me (Ps. 138:3). As the CEV translates, *"On the day I cried out, you answered me."* At times, instantly. Strength flowed daily. Fasting rather than eating to spend that time in prayer reaps powerful results!

3. Fasting coupled with prayer, brought guidance, direction, and wisdom from above. Because I gave the Lord my full attention and was ready to hear from heaven, He frequently spoke because I was listening.

4. Fasting flushes out poisons, giving our bodies time to heal themselves. It even slows the aging process. It can break the power of an uncontrollable appetite and free you from "compulsive overeating." It's been described as "spring cleaning for your body!"

> **Prayer Response:** *Lord, I now see the physical and spiritual benefits of fasting. Now, give me grace to dedicate a fast to You. I give myself to You. Help me to love You more than these things from which I fast. I seek You more than my own comfort and pleasure. With You lead-*

---
4 Rex Russell, Appendix, in Elmer L Towns, Fasting for Spiritual Breakthrough (Ventura: Regal Books, 1996) 173.

ing I am ready. Keep me strong and alert during my fast. Protect me from the Evil One, deliver me from temptation and steer my mind and heart away from all distractions. Help me to bring my spirit, soul, body, and mind into subjection and focus them on You, to Whom all praise belongs, Amen.[5]

"The Diet that Delivers"

Daniel 1:12 describes a request made by Daniel to be tested on a diet of vegetables and water instead of the rich food and wine from the king's table: *"Please test us for ten days on a diet of vegetables and water,"* Daniel said. *"At the end of the ten days, see how we look compared to the other young men who are eating the king's food. Then make your decision in light of what you see."* This passage highlights Daniel's faithfulness and trust in God's provision, even in matters of diet.

Ernest Edsel called the Daniel Diet "The diet that really delivers," underscoring the idea that a simple, plant-based diet not only sustained Daniel and his companions but also had beneficial effects. After the ten-day test, Daniel and his friends appeared healthier than those who ate the king's food, demonstrating the physical and perhaps spiritual benefits of their dietary choices.

Of all the physical/spiritual disciplines, why is fasting so difficult? Probably because it requires the crucifixion of "King Stomach." In case you haven't met him, look down and introduce yourself! You may hear him rumble in disagreement. Fasting rather than eating *to pray* reaps powerful results as we discussed! It provides visible physical and spiritual benefits. Consider the Daniel Fast. For first time fasters, "it's a type of partial fast that focuses very heavily on vegetables and other healthy whole foods but leaves out any animal sources of protein," a somewhat stricter version of the Vegan diet. The king's servants tried to feed Daniel the rich foods on the palace menu. Daniel refused. His first fast was a 10-day Vegan diet. The king's servants worried. They

---

5 The editors, "10 Inspiring Prayers for Lent and Fasting," Guideposts.

thought Daniel would get sick without the king's rich foods and drink. Daniel proved his diet worked. It kept him healthy, and he was able to accomplish great things. Prayer and fasting yields marvelous results. It gave Daniel discernment concerning which elements in the unbelieving culture God's people must simply refuse. Daniel ran the risks of faith and passed the health and appearance test with flying colors.

The Daniel diet provides physical and spiritual benefits. Elmer L. Towns writes, "The secret to a Daniel Fast is to *purpose* in your heart; that is, to make a vow as you enter the fast that you will purpose to follow the Lord in what you eat and drink." The Daniel Fast is more than a diet. It's a lifestyle. In the beginning Daniel was in trouble. He was a prisoner. He faced challenges and temptations. But he made the right choices. "Fasting brings you closer to God. It makes you more sensitive to God's voice. Fasting helps break bad habits or even addictions. Fasting shows us our weaknesses and allows us to rely on God's strength."[6]

> **Prayer Response:** *Lord, as I begin with my fast, I ask for Your blessing to help me truly experience and understand the importance of my fast, and how, just like the disciples, I can use this time to renew my faith and sharpen my focus once more. Thank you for the gift of fasting, and that I can follow this journey knowing there are so many rewards in the process. I praise You for breath, for strength, for my right mind, and especially for Your presence in my life. In Jesus' name. Amen.*[7]

Make a *"Discipline Vow"*

1 Corinthians 9:27, where Paul writes, *"…I discipline my body and bring it into subjection,"* highlights the importance of self-control and discipline in the Christian life. Paul uses the metaphor of an athlete who trains rigorously to emphasize the need for spiritual discipline.

---

6 Quotes from Dr. Josh Axe, DC, DNM, CN, "Daniel Fast: Benefits for Your Spiritual, Emotional and Physical Health," February 6, 2023.
7 I Need a Word, "Prayers to Pray When Fasting," July 23, 2023.

Elmer L. Towns calls the Daniel Fast a discipline vow that will strengthen our character in every area of our lives. The Daniel Fast, inspired by the dietary practices in the Book of Daniel, involves a commitment to a plant-based diet for a specific period. It is seen as not just a physical act of abstaining from certain foods, but as a spiritual discipline that encourages deeper focus, prayer, and reliance on God. Engaging in the Daniel Fast or similar practices can bolster one's character, foster greater spiritual awareness, and enhance one's overall commitment to living a life aligned with one's faith and values.

Ernest Edsel lost 200 lbs. in pursuit of weight loss and fitness following the diet of Daniel. His book on the Daniel diet is based on the ten-day Daniel fast, not the 21-day fast in Daniel 10. Edsel's book is built around three principles: right thinking; right eating; and right activity.[8]

1) Right Thinking. Daniel knew that right thinking was the only way he could survive and prosper as an exile in Babylon under a powerful king. When Satan controls your thoughts, he controls your life. If you, like Daniel, are under a lot of pressure and stress at home or work, right thinking is essential and fasting can help. Dr. Axe concurs, "It is a spiritual discipline that requires denying your physical and mental self because your stomach and your brain will most likely work overtime to remind you when and what they want to eat!"

2) Right Eating. Daniel knew that right eating was the only way he could keep his faith and do good works. You will not go hungry eating the right foods. Eliminate sugar, bread, flour. Eat lots of vegetables and drink plenty of pure water. If you are addicted to sugar as I was, fasting helps break that addiction. "If you need to bring "the flesh off the throne," Jentezen Franklin recommends that "when we fast, we submit our bodies to God and say, 'Cleanse this body, and deal with the habits and other things that are earthly.'"

---

8 Ernest Edsel, The Diet of Daniel (Lincoln: Writers Club Press, 2002).

3) Right Living. In the end Daniel became a ruler. Kings came to him for advice. He was pure enough to receive revelations from God. Don't just fast. Fast and pray and spend a lot of time in God's Word. When crises came Daniel didn't pray more nor pray less; he continued his excellent prayer and fasting life (Dan.6:10-13). My prayer for you would be that God would develop in you "a gentle kindness," following Jesus who was gentle and compassionate. If hungry makes you angry, well, you're "Hangry," and you can't develop right living without being kind to everybody.

> **Prayer Response:** *Father, by your Spirit working in me, empower me to take control of my inner character. Empower me with self-discipline as I do my work. Help me change my bad habits and to quit the excuses. I want to think right, eat right, and above all live right. Make me a more disciplined person in all areas of my life. I ask for your strength as I start small and grow out of my areas of weakness. Show me what I need to change in my thinking, my eating habits, but especially in the way I live my life. I don't want to be the same. Make me the best version of myself possible. In Jesus' name. Amen.*

God Came to Town

Years ago, the order was given that Protestants could no longer hold meetings in Osaka, Japan. Officials resisted all attempts to rescind the ban. Two Christian leaders did the only thing knew to do—pray and fast! At the prayer meeting in defiance of the order to cease the meetings, the Spirit of God came down. Two sons of city officials went to altar and were saved. The next morning, the leaders got word, "Go on with your meetings; you will not be interrupted. Imagine the headline in the newspaper the next morning: "The Christians' God came to town last night."

Don't you long to see God come your town? Desperation and urgency should drive us to prayer and fasting. Hungry people aren't "hangry," but desperate people. When we are hungry in the flesh, we become hungry in spirit. How *desperate* for answers, hope and change are you? Desperate prayer and fasting seems so simple but is rarely done by many of us. Fasting and prayer produce a fresh reliance on God. The issue is that even within the church, we often seek answers and solutions in methods and human efforts, rather than turning to God.

> **Prayer Response:** *Father, You see my desperation, my urgency, and my lack of patience. I don't always see things the way You do. Give me your perspective on things. You tell us not to fear and You draw us close into your Presence. You're the only place we find refuge in the storms that surround us right now, Lord. You're the only place we can find peace and strength. So, I ask You for your words of truth and power to strengthen me in my inner being and lift my heart to You. Help me to trust in You. Rescue me and answer me, and I will raise a banner of victory in Your name, Lord God. Enable me to stand firm when the foundations are shaking. You are my God, my Redeemer, and You are mighty to save. In Jesus mighty name. Amen.*

"God's Nuclear Option"

In Isaiah 58:5 God questions the sincerity of fasting when it is done superficially, highlighting that true fasting should reflect genuine humility and a commitment to justice. Jentezen Franklin emphasizes the spiritual rewards of fasting, stating that it brings individuals closer to God and that no reward is greater than this deepened connection. Together, these perspectives underscore that fasting should not be a mere ritual but a meaningful discipline that fosters a closer relationship with God and reflects a sincere heart aligned with His will.

For seven years (2007 to 2014) the Southern Florida District was called to the Daniel Fast to bring in the New Year. I cannot speak for the scores of people who joined me, but I can testify to the truth of Franklin's affirmation. Prayer and fasting strike the winning blows so the result is big kingdom successes. Dr. Towns indicates that "Scripture ties fasting and revival together. As believers fast and pray, God sends revival to His people." He also insists, "Find an approach to fasting that will accomplish holy purposes in your own life and in the lives of those you love."[9]

Some of the crises you face can only be overcome by God's power. If, for example, your church is "like a ship taking on water," you're listing. Don't be overwhelmed. Seek the Lord's face in prayer and deny yourself by fasting. Don't be disheartened. Discover the power of fasting to see the breakthrough you so desperately need. Yes, even in those stubborn areas you struggle the most to change. I agree with Rhoda Faye Diehl, that it's time to fight back with fasting, "God's secret weapon against the enemy's strongholds. Jesus even said that some evil spirits cannot be cast out except by prayer and fasting, KJV. That should tell us a lot about the power of this weapon—it's basically God's nuclear option."[10]

Elmer L. Towns, in his insightful book, *Fasting for Spiritual Breakthrough,* reviews nine biblical fasts, but warns his readers before anyone would think about embarking on any fast, biblical, or not, to "consult your physician before beginning." Certain medical conditions and problems require some of us to remain on "essential diets." Rest assured, "God would not command a physical exercise that would harm people physically or emotionally," even though it may seem that everyone can and should fast. Type 2 Diabetes Miletus all but eliminated fasting for me. Hopefully, it won't for you.

Prayer Response: *Heavenly Father, in your powerful name, Mountains shake and seas roar. At your name, creation sings with joy. At your name, demons flee. At your name, every knee will bow, and every tongue confess that you are Lord. In your powerful name. I pray for the breakthrough I need, believing there is no power greater than*

---
9 Elmer L. Towns, Fasting for Spiritual Breakthrough, 62.
10 Rhoda Faye Diehl, "Prayer and Fasting for Breakthrough," Called Writers Christian Publishing.

your name. Unleash your power in my life in the powerful name of Jesus, my Savior and Lord, Amen.

Why Don't We Fast?

Somebody said, "Fasting without prayer is starvation." Fasting must be accompanied by prayer to maintain its spiritual purpose, transforming it from mere abstinence into a meaningful practice. Sincere seeking (prayer) and fasting are essential for spiritual growth and connection with God (Heb.11:6b).

Fasting is not in vogue, at least in churches in the West. The idea of 21st century Christians fasting seems bizarre. Why would a person deliberately starve himself or herself like the ascetics in medieval times? Why do so few Christians fast, which for Jesus in Matthew 6, was one of the big three spiritual disciplines? Among great Bible saints who fasted were Moses the lawgiver, David the king, Elijah the prophet, and Daniel the seer.

In the New Testament we have the example of our Lord as well as of His apostles. Fasting clearly had its place in the life of some of the Bible's most notable heroes. Could it be as Arthur Wallis intimates, "A new day is dawning, and a new thirst for the Spirit is beginning to awaken the slumbering Church?"[11] Prayer *and* fasting releases the power of God in His Church. God not only sustains but gives wisdom and direction to those who seek Him through fasting. It is known that all the most intense forms of prevailing prayer can be substantially deepened, clarified, and greatly empowered through the practice of fasting.

Prayer demands times seasons of solitude in which we shut out the world and seek diligently after God. Fasting intensifies such seeking times. When God is our exclusive concern, not food for a specified period, He rewards us with something as simple as breaking from our world's rhythm and demands. Diehl again, "When we fast, we are acknowledging that we need spiritual help. We are humbling ourselves and acknowledging that we cannot solve our own problem. We're ac-

---
11 Arthur Wallis, God's Chosen Fast (Fort Washington: CLC Publications, 2007 printing) 12-13.

knowledging that the natural isn't enough, and that we need to tap into the spiritual."[12] Could it be we have not because we fast not?

> **Prayer Response:** *Father, I open my heart to you asking You to release your power in my life and in my church. If I cannot fast for medical reasons show me how best to intensify my prayer efforts. But if I can fast, I ask You to help me embrace fasting as a means of grace to express my spiritual commitment to You and to strengthen my connection to You. Trigger fresh new hope that my circumstances will improve as I humble myself through this means of self-denial and prevailing prayer. In the powerful name of Jesus I pray, Amen.*

"You've-Gotta-be-Kidding-Me"

In Matthew 9:14, the disciples of John the Baptist question Jesus about why His disciples do not fast like they and the Pharisees do. This interaction serves as a reminder that fasting should be a personal action with a specific purpose, rather than a ritualistic display of piety. True fasting is about genuine spiritual intention, emphasizing authenticity and heartfelt devotion rather than outward appearances. John's disciples noticed that Jesus' disciples did not fast. Jesus responds that fasting isn't required (commanded) and should never become a routine ritual with no other purpose than to be seen of people.

The Pharisees had a propensity for wrong motives and legalistic ritual (Matt. 6). Later, Jesus called them *"blind guides that strain out a gnat but swallow a camel"* (Matt. 23:24, NIV). They picked a fine time to bring up the subject of fasting after feasting at Matthew's table (Matt. 9:10). They asked a "you-gotta-be-kidding-me" question and Jesus answers with a "never-to-be-forgotten" question of His own: *"Do wedding guests mourn while celebrating with the groom? Of course not. But someday the groom will be taken away from them, and then they will fast"* (Matt.9:15, NLT). Fasting may be observed at appropriate times, but not at a wedding reception when the groom is present. He's right

---
12 Rhoda Faye Diehl, "Prayer and Fasting for Breakthrough."

here. Enjoy His presence. Jesus is with his disciples just as the wedding guests are with the groom. Think celebration, not deprivation. Enjoy the relationship; absorb his teaching; follow His example while you can. Refuse to be shamed, intimidated, or condemned by any unstated disapproval. Never settle for religion when Christ offers an intimate relationship.

The Teacher commanded no one to fast. "Fasting can be beneficial; but I don't think we should fast legalistically in ritual piety,"[13] as the Pharisees. He knew times were coming when His disciples would fast. I simply ask you consider fasting as an essential spiritual practice. Some may never fast, but those who do so will soon see the many benefits. WebMD suggests, "If you're thinking of trying a fast and you have diabetes, you'll want to know what the risks are, how to avoid them, and you should check with your doctor first."

> **Prayer Response:** *Father, as I begin this fast You know that I desire to be near You every moment to receive the joy that is waiting for me. Hold my hand, guide me, and let me live in Your perfect will. Wrap Your Spirit around me, so my every breath is in sequence with Yours. Let peace envelop my thoughts and encompass my body. May I never, ever pull away. In Jesus' awesome name. I pray. Amen.*[14]

Fasting Increases Spiritual Sensitivity

In 2 Samuel 12:16, David's fasting and prayer for his child highlight the personal and sincere nature of fasting. It's a reminder that fasting is not about setting records or competing with others, but rather about earnestly seeking God with humility.

---

13 Tim Chastain, "Jesus Refuses to Ask his Disciples to Fast," Jesus Without Baggage, October 19, 2015.
14 Adapted from ConnectUS, "10 Powerful Prayers for Joy," July 14, 2021.

When God draws you to fast, know why you are fasting and create a focus for your fast. When considering a fast, there are several questions you should ask. "What are you interested in? Are you interested in eating right? Losing weight? Getting fit? Staying healthy?"[15] If so, fasting can get you started on the road back to health and fitness. Do you seek "a closer walk with God?" We've reviewed some of the spiritual reasons why we should fast. Why are you feeling drawn to fast? David fasted for a specific purpose, the health of his child.

Paul and Ruth Anne came to me for advice about fasting because they felt drawn to it spiritually. Instantly, I suggested the Daniel Fast because I knew it was "The Diet that Delivers" outstanding benefits. This encouraged them to go forward in their very first fast. I prayed for God's power to be released through their fasting. Like most of us, they described themselves as "lovers of food." A diet of only fruits, vegetables, and whole grains "rocked (their) world." They would learn how much they relied on comfort food and how often food regularly crossed their minds.

"The rewards of observing a fast," observes Dr. Russell, "include spiritual, mental and physical benefits," the least of which are "a very valuable way to experience the divine design for total health." They were about to see how fasting added a new engine to their lives. It helped to clarify their priorities and increased their spiritual sensitivity. They learned how vital fasting was to their walk with God. "Your spiritual sensitivity is something that you can increase from time to time," and fasting is a means of grace that expands "your ability to pick up spiritual information and signals from heaven. "The more sensitive you are to the realm of the Spirit, the more victory you will enjoy… you will avoid a lot of mistakes and blunders that people do just because of their dullness in the things of God."[16]

Prayer Response: *Lord, as I begin this time of fasting, fill me with your strength. Help me to use this as a time*

---
15 Edsel, xi.
16 Pastor Victor, "Fasting Increases Your Spiritual Sensitivity," Grace Plus Church, December 28, 2018.

of growth, renewal, and healing. Calm my anxiety about what giving up food and the discomfort that I might face. Help me focus not on what is being taken away, but what I'm gaining as I use this as a spiritual discipline. With you leading, Holy Spirit, I am ready. Amen.

A Report from the Fasting Frontline

Paul and Ruth Anne Flowers contacted me for guidance as they felt called to embark upon a Daniel Fast. Ruth Anne is a high school teacher, so her day is packed with hardly any breaks. While working, the Daniel Fast was ever on her mind. "My stomach would growl, and I'd think about lunch. When I'd remember what was in my lunch box, I'd pray. When I'd reach for a snack of fruits or nuts, I'd pray. I'd pray for my husband and me, for our marriage, for our children, for wisdom, for peace. And God granted it all. He granted it in abundance." She discovered what you will discover: you are not too busy to incorporate a fast into a busy schedule.

On the first morning of her 21-day fast, Ruth Anne said, "I prayed out loud, 'Lord, in your name, please release me from this spirit of anxiety and depression.' That moment was an instant release of pressure on my chest. It was the first morning, and God was already delivering me." She continued, "Overwhelming depression was overtaking me." Dealing with stress related to difficulties within your family can put a great deal of pressure on your marriage and family. She found herself crying each night... "sinking more deeply." Deliverance brought freedom and joy. Every child of God has a right to enjoy the benefits of deliverance from the things that have been defeating. Jesus takes you out of the kingdom of enslavement and makes you a citizen of a heavenly kingdom, you are free. You now have the power to choose to live in holiness and in righteousness before God. There is no greater freedom than this. Gina Smith offers some great advice: "If you're feeling depressed, remember that you're not alone. God is with you always. Don't be afraid to reach out to people in your family, your church, or your friend circles. Ask them to pray with and for you, and continue to pray each day, asking God to draw you closer to Himself."[17]

> **Prayer Response:** *Heavenly Father, I am grateful that you are stable, even when I feel like I am sinking. Right now, my brain and emotions are telling me that something isn't right. It feels like Satan has been whipping me around! Please sustain me, protect me, and enable me to stand. You are bringing deliverance, freedom and joy from the things that were defeating me. Please help me as I sift through my circumstances to see if there is a need for change in some way. Come alongside me, wrap Your arms of love around me, and help me walk until I am strong enough to walk confidently on my own. How I praise You for perseverance to stick with it and reap the benefits of this dedicated fast. In the mighty name of Jesus, Amen.*[18]

No Walk in the Park

Ruth Anne heard the challenge to fast while on her commute to school. "When you're down," you usually take it out on the one you love most," she confessed. She had participated in a 30-hour famine as a teenager but "had never truly participated in a time of fasting… a time of true sacrifice." She'd given up certain pleasures before for the Lenten season, but "knew in her heart of hearts, that she needed something greater." "Fasting is an ancient practice of the Church; at its best, it is an authentic exercise in trust and a quiet form of deep devotion. It joins us to Christ and to one another. Fasting—in whatever form it takes—is nothing less than a participation in the transforming cross of Jesus Christ, which is the goal of every worthwhile Lenten journey."[19]

Accepting the challenge to fast is no "walk in the park." Fasting is an

---
[17] Gina Smith, "Healing Prayers for Battling Depression and Scriptures to Ease Anxiety," Crosswalk, May 7, 2024.
[18] Gleaned from Gina Smith, "Healing Prayers for When You Battle Depression," Crosswalk.com, May 4, 2017.
[19] Amy Ekeh, "10 Reasons to Fast This Lent," St. Anthony Messenger, March 2019.

"in-your-face statement to the devil that he isn't going to win." Expect the enemy to be hard at work as you fast, but as Ruth Anne testified, "He didn't win, and he won't!" As she journeyed through those days, she studied the book of Daniel. This verse stood out to her. Nebuchadnezzar asked for his dream to be interpreted, but when the magicians and astrologers asked, "What dream?" Nebuchadnezzar replied, "You tell me." "No one can reveal it to the king except the gods, and they do not live among humans. *The gods do not live among humans."* Out loud Ruth Anne affirmed, "Oh yes He does! Our God lives in us. He lives with us, and when we're weak, He is strong!" After all, "Jesus' nickname is Immanuel–God with us." Keep walking this "God-with-us life"[20] no matter how difficult it gets. Ruth Anne discovered anew that walking with God means to be in harmony with Him as she journeyed through life. She determined that she would listen to His commandments, put her faith in Him, and work to follow His path for her. She was freeing herself of things that distracted or burdened her. Looking back on the experience Ruth Anne reported, "Throughout my fast, God reminded me that He does live with us. He gave us increased strength, and those 21 days are still blessing my life."

> **Prayer Response:** *Father, I bend my knee and receive new insight on Your truth. I open my ears to receive Your counsel. I open my heart to receive Your eternal wisdom. May your words be like a lamp that lights my path. May your love be like a compass that gives me direction. May your truth be like a signpost bringing clarity.*[21] *Amen.*

"God Leans in a Little Closer"

Does your soul thirst for God (Psalm 42:1)? He is the catalyst for every righteous cause. "But when you fast and pray," Tony Hall said, "God leans in a little closer."[22] And when you have a concentrated focus for your fast on a pinpointed need, miracles happen. The book

---

20 Gospel Conversations, Brentwood Baptist Church blog, "Two Reasons Prayer is Essential to Making Disciples with Jesus." February 19, 2023.
21 Drawn heavily from "Prayer for Wisdom," lords-prayer-words.com.
22 Quoted in Batterson, If, 46.

of Acts explodes with miraculous power. Powerful demonstrations of thirst-quenching intimacy come from fasting and prayer. We are content when "there's nothing on earth we desire except God" alone. We seem to desire many things. But living with a sense of dependence on God alone satisfies the deepest longings of our souls and will bring us joyful contentment.

Ruth Anne's husband, Paul, joined Ruth Anne in the Daniel Fast. A song based on St. Teresa of Avila's prayer played over and over in his heart on the first day of their 21-day journey: "Patience obtains all things / Whoever has God lacks nothing / God alone suffices." They found themselves drinking at the stream of God's active presence even on their morning commute. Those who long for God are never disappointed because He seems to lean in a little closer to those seek Him. When we fast, it seems that we are leaning into Him for help and comfort and not on our own understanding. Learn to lean and you will discover God is leaning in closer because you are desperate for Him. He especially takes note that our hunger for Him has surpassed our hunger for anything else. "Fasting helps us realize our dependence on God for our physical needs and brings us a deeper appreciation of His Word. Some situations only change when we fast and pray (Matt. 17:21)."[23]

> **Prayer Response:** *Lord, I thirst for You. I need refreshing, new life to surge within me to satisfy my thirst and give me newness of life as I drink at Your fountain. Grant me a good long draught from the cool spring of living water that makes me never thirst again (John 4:14). Make me an oak of righteousness planted by streams of water, whose leaves do not wither. Bless me according to Your perfect will, as You watch over my way. Show me Your power and the glory of Your great love. In Jesus' name. Amen.*

---

[23] Evangelist L. Parsons, "How Can Fasting Bring You Closer to Christ," Church Blog News, June 11, 2020.

Revitalize Your Prayer Life

In the parched wilderness of our lives, where we thirst for spiritual renewal, *Psalm 63:1* reminds us, "You, God, are my God; earnestly I seek you. My whole being longs for you in a dry and parched land where there is no water." Fasting deepens this quest, enhancing our prayer life and opening doors to extraordinary divine interventions. As Paul experienced, fasting brings us into a closer state of openness and communion with God, where receiving His revelations and responding through intercession become a natural extension of our spiritual journey. Time and again, the Lord showed me that when we were open to listening, he would speak." Does your marriage or family need healing? It's true, "Marriage doesn't take two people; it takes three." You've tried everything else. Make God the center of your marriage. Try prayer and fasting. Paul testifies,

> *"(God) melded Ruth Anne's and my heart together and we naturally found a method of addressing a few issues, which began this season of prayer. We had clarity on how to interact with the children, how to approach things at work and how to be better spouses one to another."*

When I asked for Paul's biggest takeaway from the Daniel Fast, he responded, "If I cultivate a heart of prayer, then I'm more aware, even in mundane tasks, of how God's presence (permeates) even (the) minor moments of life. I look forward to seeing how God uses this (awakened) awareness of His presence as we move forward in prayer." Even if we have prayed our whole lives, some of us have hardly scratched the surface of God's love and intention for prayer. Do you long to make prayer more than a conversation with a distant father? Then make prayer the foundation of your faith. Get to know Him on a heart-to-heart basis. Prayer and fasting opens the door to the transformation you seek. "Take time to open the door to the Lord's healing hand. If it is hard to trust, start small. He will reward you as you offer all that you are able. There is power in prayer. Prayer is one of our greatest weapons against Satan who is out to destroy marriages and families. When we spend time in prayer, God provides us the strength to stand up to the lies of the enemy and open the door to transformation."[24]

> **Prayer Response:** *Father, I pray for unity in my marriage today. "Give us the ability to be a united front for you letting nothing come between us. Help us, Father to identify and work through anything that is not pleasing to you so we can continually reach higher levels of unity in our marriage – spiritually, physically, and mentally."*[25] *In Jesus' name. Amen.*

Exceeding All Expectations

Mark Batterson wrote, "One of two things happens over time. Either your theology will conform to your reality, and your expectations will get smaller and smaller until you can hardly believe God for anything. Or your reality will conform to your theology, and your expectations will get bigger and bigger until you can believe God for absolutely everything."[26]

In 2009, our district-wide Daniel Fast focused on God's provision for our people, our local churches, and our district in those difficult days of recession and financial crisis. Fasting brought miraculous answers to prayer. In December 2008, the financial report showed district funds were minus $100,000 in arrears. By April, the church year ended in the black. Whitney Hopler acknowledges, "If you're struggling with financial problems, you may feel overwhelmed. Maybe you've prayed for God's help but haven't yet experienced solutions. Adding fasting to your prayers can bring about breakthroughs in even the toughest situations. As you fast, God can change your perspective to reveal His plan more clearly for your finances."[27]

---

24 Nicole Kauffman, "Cultivating a Heart of Prayer," Courage. Hope. Love., January 23, 2017.
25 Michael and Carlie Kercheval, "20 Marriage Prayers for A Stronger, Healthier Relationship," Crosswalk.com, October 5, 2021.
26 Batterson, Whisper, 114.
27 Whitney Hopler, "Prayer and Fasting for a Financial Breakthrough," Crosswalk.com, March 5, 2007.

In 2010, we fasted and prayed for a real movement of the Holy Spirit in every local church resulting in revival, evangelism, and discipleship. During that "Acts 2 Awakening," over 2,000 believers sought the renewing, cleansing, infilling of the Holy Spirit. We asked God for two thousand to be added by profession of faith. God gave us 1,600, the highest ever recorded in a single year. Aim high. Ask largely of God. Then don't be surprised when He exceeds every expectation. When we are effectively fasting, we are creating an environment for miracles. He can do it in us or through us if we make room for Him to intervene in our circumstances. When we engage in fasting and prayer, we embark on a journey of spiritual alignment—an opportunity to see ourselves and our circumstances through God's eyes. It's a transformative experience that allows us to discern His perspective and purpose in our lives.

Consider the power of this divine insight. When we view our challenges as God sees them, we recognize His sovereignty and the potential for His intervention. Our perspective shifts from one of hopelessness to one of hopeful anticipation, trusting in His promises. This reorientation can be life-changing, helping us to understand that the victories God has in store are beyond our current comprehension.

In moments of deep need, when we feel overburdened by life's demands, remember this: God's victories often look different from our expectations. They are more profound, far-reaching, and transformative than we can imagine. As you persist in prayer and fasting, remain open to His guidance, and you may begin to perceive the victories He is preparing, not only for your immediate needs but for the larger story He's writing through your life.

Trust that His plans for you are good, as Jeremiah 29:11 affirms. May this journey of seeking Him lead to victories that truly exceed your imagination and affirm His power at work in your life.

Prayer Response: *Help us to see our finances through Your eyes. You have a purpose and plan for our lives, and every cent we're blessed with to manage. Stir our hearts to seek Your counsel on everything from buying dessert to* *a brand-new car. Urge us to seek You in Your Word, and prayerfully consider Jesus' example on this earth. We confess that we don't often stop to think about what You want for our wallet over what we want. When new trends are just a swipe of the credit card away, stir in our hearts to fight temptation."* [28] *In Jesus' name. Amen.*

Fasting Accelerates Answered Prayer

I believe that fasting and prayer together unleash a unique supernatural power that is unparalleled in its impact. Mahesh Chavda once said, "We don't fast to earn something; we fast to make a connection with our supernatural God. We are cleaning out the 'pipe' that connects us to the anointing of God." If we really want God to work mightily in our homes, our families, and our churches, we must humble ourselves and seek his face through prayer and fasting. Going into our secret place of prayer; bowing our heads and hearts like little children; and crying out to God for fresh new mercies and grace, puts us in miracle territory.

If it's been a while, it's time to set aside your normal routine and seek the face of God. Say no to food for a specified period to say yes to God. Confess your need and let your desire for Him be more than for food itself. Fasting is a sure way to humble yourself before God. When we humble ourselves grace flows down to the humble (1 Pet. 5:5-6). Don't let fasting be the one thing lacking—the one thing that keeps the free flow of God's miraculous power to transform the troubles you see. Desolate, barren lives—lives destroyed by drugs, alcohol, illicit sex, and brokenness—can be transformed. "Put God to the test when troubles come," admonished Billy Graham. It may seem far beyond the realm of possibility from a human point of view, but God specializes in redemption and transformation (see Isaiah 58). This is why we fast! Supernatural results please God. You might even begin to see accelerated answers to prayer at "lightning speed" (Isa. 65:24).

---

28 Ibid., Hopler.

As Natalie Nichols emphasizes, "Prayer is the hand that grabs the invisible. Fasting is the hand by which we let go of the visible. Prayer is the way we reach out for God and the unseen realm. Fasting is the way we let go of everything that can be seen and touched."[29] What we eat matters and fasting may bring health benefits but fasting does wonders for the soul and pushes us into miracle territory.

> **Prayer Response:** *"God of the universe, thank you that you have plans for me that are for my good and your glory. Your word says that you are the God who performs miracles: you display your power among the people. With your mighty arm, you redeemed your people and rescued them from their distress. Perform miracles in my life Lord to display your power and glory. Increase my faith to trust in you. May my whole spirit and soul and body be kept blameless to the end. Through Jesus Christ, our Lord, Amen."* [30]

---

[29] Natalie Nichols, "Fasting Day 9: Feeding Faith, Part Two," Shades of Grace Ministries, January 21, 2011.
[30] ConnectUS, "31 Powerful Prayers For Miracles to Happen," September 20, 2020.

8

Expanding Your Faith Horizon

"Prayer wonderfully clears the vision; steadies the nerves; defines duty; stiffens the purpose; sweetens and strengthens the spirit," S.D. Gordon once articulated, emphasizing the enriching effects of prayer on our being. Coupled with the insights from our days spent focusing on the physical, mental, emotional, and spiritual benefits of fasting, it becomes evident that some prayers, by nature and scope, brush the edge of impossibility. In this vein, it is crucial not to limit oneself only to the endeavors stamped with 'possible,' but to venture courageously into the realms of the seemingly impossible, bolstered by the combined powers of prayer and fasting.

With a little human effort, we can accomplish those, especially if we move out of inactivity and are not lazy as Adalberto Herrera charged. My week in Kigali, Rwanda, birthed a vision to begin praying Extraordinary Prayer Requests (EPRs), things so big and bold, so audacious and utterly impossible, that I could barely believe God would answer them. As will be shown, any time we use words like "all, each, or every," instead of "one, some, many or most," we've crossed into miracle terrain. Who prays like this? Well, I met a courageous man of faith who changed the way I prayed. Perhaps God will expand your faith horizon to include the extraordinary. It just might make an eternal difference.

Prayer Response: *God, You have all power and authority, and there's nothing we can ask you to do that You do not have all power to accomplish. Nothing is beyond you. You could say the word and do it right now. Increase our faith to believe all things are possible with You.[1] In Jesus' powerful name, Amen.*

Vision Has a Birthplace

In the Thursday afternoon session amid sweltering heat, Dr. Eugenio Duarte, then Africa Regional Director, challenged leaders in that 2007 Rwanda conference to join him in praying *"Ten Extraordinary Prayer Requests"* for the continent of Africa. What he could never have envisioned was the far-reaching impact of the vision he shared. Jentezen Franklin taught that "every assignment God gives you has a birthplace." Then he asks, "What will He reveal today?"[2] This. Every vision has a birthplace too. I needed to pray and fast for a purpose. I had begun to embrace fasting as a spiritual discipline. Was God now showing me that fasting is for the impossible? Had I providentially been led to embrace this ancient spiritual regimen known as fasting?

As Pastor Adalberto Herrera fervently prayed for a divine "anointing of multiplication," hoping to amplify his impact by focusing deeply on a select few, a striking realization washed over me: his prayers were being answered right before our eyes. Under his guidance, thirty-four leaders had emerged, each equipped and inspired to educate at least 500 others across the French Equatorial District. Witnessing this profound expansion of influence, I felt compelled to adopt this transformative approach. With enthusiastic support from Dr. Duarte, I too began seeking "Extraordinary Prayer Requests" (EPRs) to invoke similar miraculous growth in Southern Florida. The ripple effect of this powerful prayer was just beginning to unfold.

---

1 Adapted from David Platt, "Increase our Faith (Luke 17:5–6)," Radical, March 3, 2023.
2 Franklin, Fasting Journal, 54.

UNLEASHING THE SUPERNATURAL

In the invigorating aftermath of the Kigali conference, a profound desire took hold of me as I journeyed to a church board meeting on the West Coast. While embracing a period of fasting, I felt a deep yearning to connect with my own unique set of Extraordinary Prayer Requests (EPRs). With my heart open and my mind clear, I began to receive these divine inspirations as I navigated the scenic route from Lake Placid to Bradenton, Florida, a stretch of about 85 miles.

As my car hummed along the northern path, ideas began to crystallize. I hastily scribbled them on a notepad perched on the armrest, each thought flowing smoothly onto paper. By the time I reached the quaint town of Zolfo Springs on Highway 66, four distinct EPRs had been divinely bestowed upon me. The journey continued to be fruitful, with the next six revelations occurring just before I crossed under Interstate 75 on Highway 64.

Although some of these prayer requests required refinement, I felt an overwhelming sense of guidance from the Spirit. By the end of my journey, I had a personal list of ten Extraordinary Prayer Requests, each a beacon guiding my faith and work forward in remarkable new ways.

You don't have to be nearly as ambitious. Perhaps God will give you only two or three impossible EPRs, things that only God can do. Such huge, targeted requests will expand your faith and enable you to get the most out of your disciplined effort in prayer and fasting. David Livingstone informs us: "Fastings and vigils without a special object in view are time run to waste." In other words, know your reason for fasting and pray with targeted requests.[3] EPRs evoke extreme wonder. When God "speaks, entire worlds are thrown into motion."

Prayer Response: *Father, open my spiritual eyes to see your mysteries, bring me into deep and intimate knowledge of your world and your ways, and enable me to grasp the vision that You have for me, and may I be sensitive to Your leading and guidance. Grant me a clear vision and lead me along the right path I ask in Jesus' name. Amen.*

---
3 Quoted in Grace Fox, "Fasting for a Purpose," August 13, 2019.

Pray BHAG Prayers

Matthew 19:26 reminds us of the limitless possibilities when we align ourselves with God's power. However, as Aaron Berry points out, this promise isn't a guarantee for personal desires to be fulfilled like a good luck charm. Instead, it encourages trust in God's greater plan and the possibilities that arise from faith and spiritual alignment with His will. Fasting is not a good luck charm like the power of positive thinking, but some prayers are so far beyond anything we can think or imagine, they can only be achieved by God to whom nothing is impossible. Prayer and fasting prompts you to pray extraordinary vision prayers—Big. Holy. Audacious. Goals. And live by faith. Consider the list God gave me:

1. Every believer a Spirit-filled Christ-like disciple.
2. Every believer a disciple maker with a real burden for lost people.
3. Every home a training center for holiness champions.
4. Every believer mobilized to prayer and fasting.
5. Every leader in sync with biblical priorities: God, family, church.
6. Every leader mentoring leaders who mentor other leaders.
7. Every pastor a Spirit-anointed and effective preacher of the Word.
8. Every local church a ministry outpost offering home, help and hope.
9. Every local church excelling in the grace of giving.
10. Every local church experiencing a real movement of the Holy Spirit in revival.

These were BHAGs—Big. *Holy*. Audacious. Goals.[4] When we fast and pray believing all things are possible with God, we are yielding ourselves to his sovereign plan, trusting Him to do big things only

---
4 Jim Collins and Jerry Porras, Built to Last: Successful Habits of Visionary Companies (New York: Harper Collins Publishers, Inc.) 1994.

He can do. When we pray and fast, nothing is impossible. Miracles happen.

> **Prayer Response:** *Dear heavenly Father, thank you for the assurance of your steadfast love, fresh new mercies, and goals that are borderline impossible. Since nothing is impossible to you, I am primed with a prayer for a miracle to happen in even the hardest situations. Now Lord, with palms up, I praise You and surrender to You—the God who does all things well and who makes all things beautiful, in your time. Amen.[5]*

Stretching BHAG's

As has been noted, anytime the words "every" or "all," are attached to our prayers, it means every single person or church. At best, it is a bit of a stretch. Leaders tend to think in majority terms and congratulate themselves if they can get 51% of their people doing anything. Our sense of success is often tied to how many people are motivated to do what we envision. While you are thinking big, why not pray big? I can only imagine what might happen if the percentages climbed to the sixties or seventies and beyond. What if we stopped trying to work and do things for God and start doing things *from* God?

Look closer at my Big Holy Audacious Goals and you will see that they started with the individual because that's where any change must start. But it's even more personal than that. "For things to change, Gandhi forewarned, "first *I* must change." Personalize your list. It doesn't have to be ten as discussed! Remember I was thinking in terms of my assignment as a leader over close to one hundred churches. Don't copy; let the Spirit create.

Don't let the number ten scare you away. Begin to envision as many God-sized goals as He wants you to believe for, even if only three or five or seven. The point is, ask the Holy Spirit to give you com-

---
[5] Adapted from Scotty Smith, "A Prayer for Trusting God in Seemingly Impossible Situations," March 9, 2015.

pellingly audacious prayer goals that are so far beyond you, that they stretch you and may only come about by prayer and fasting. Batterson calls such prayers our "bravest prayers," the ones that you can barely believe God for because they are so impossible.[6] If we are hungry for God to do the impossible, we must fast and pray like we believe it.

Here's a good way to pray for the impossible: "Lord, "even the winds and waves obey your command. When I feel weak and limited, I will put my trust in You and remember that your power is limitless. When my problems feel impossible, I will hand them over to You, for whom all things are possible. Amen."[7]

> **Prayer Response:** *Lord, I acknowledge my faith and belief in your power to do miraculous things, even though most of time I ask for things we can accomplish together empowered by Your Holy Spirit. Forgive me for the times I've said, "I've got this!" when should have acknowledged You as my source of power and strength. I know You hear my prayers and want me ask largely of You. Increase my faith to believe for bigger and better things. This is new territory for me, Lord, daring to pray what seems humanly impossible. But you are a God who makes a way where there is no way, the God of impossible possibilities and I ask in your powerful name. Jesus. Amen.*

Depend On God Alone

At the very heart of our faith, dependence on God should be the primary pursuit for every believer. His omnipotent power surpasses all that we can request or conceive, meeting not only our profoundest longings but also our most critical needs. The remarkable testament of this truth was vividly illustrated during our time with the African leaders in Kigali—none of whom possessed even the simplest luxury of a car, nor did they carry luggage filled for a long journey. Yet, their

---

6 Mark Batterson, The Bravest Prayer, March 7, 2020.
7 Kathryn Shirey, "Daily Prayer for the Impossible," Prayer + Possibilities, August 12, 2019.

circumstances framed a powerful lesson: "Depend upon God alone; not on financial support, nor on others dictating every step."

We fervently prayed that these African pastors would embrace a robust independence, anchored not in material abundance but in spiritual richness. With inspiring confidence tempered by humility, one pastor captured the essence of their faith: "We do not possess wealth, but we hold something far greater—a God whose resources and possibilities exceed our wildest imaginations." This profound declaration not only served as a beacon of inspiration but also a call to deeper faith, urging us all to look beyond our visible means and trust in the boundless provision of God.

Self-reliance is a lie because we "live in a web of dependence," wrote Philip Yancey, "at the center of which is God in whom all things hold together."[8] We will never outgrow dependence, and to the extent we think we do, we delude ourselves. Take a bite of this wisdom: "Dependence on God means we need Him, and we understand that without Him we are unable to accomplish anything of Kingdom significance."[9]

Stop comparing yourself with others. Focus on your own growth and progress. It is foolish to compare yourself with those who are gifted with greater opportunities and resources as an excuse for not doing what God has called you to do. "Too much comparison leads to unhappiness and low self-esteem. We become frustrated with ourselves for "not being good enough," or angry with others," counsels Elizabeth Perry.[10] Our emphasis should be on the gifts we have received from God. Pursuing BHAGs (Big Holy Audacious Goals) typically requires us to transition from a mindset of independence to one of interdependence. To successfully achieve these lofty goals, particularly when we rely on the support of others, mastering the skill of collaboration is crucial. This ability ensures that our collective efforts are effectively channeled towards accomplishing shared objectives.

---
8 Philip Yancey, Prayer: Does It Make Any Difference?" 34.
9 Boyd Bailey, "Depend on God," Wisdom Hunters, March 13, 2012.
10 Elizabeth Perry, "Stop Comparing Yourself to Others…" Better Up, February 8, 2022.

Prayer Response: *Help me, Lord, to acknowledge my total dependence on You at this moment. I need your help. I pray that you'd help me live dependently on your help. I need your help daily. I give you my time and my devotion, my hours of solitude. Grant me a keen sense of Your presence as I practice hour-by-hour dependence on You. Convict me whenever I go my own way, or I compare myself with others. I give myself to You in fresh commitment and surrender. In the strong name Amen.*

Discover Your Best Possible Version

"Every believer a Spirit-filled disciple" is indeed a motivating goal for any denomination. House cleaning is done with the purpose of making it a welcoming and livable space. This can signify preparing oneself internally and spiritually, ensuring that one's spiritual house is clean, orderly, and ready to be filled with the Holy Spirit, akin to making a physical home suitable for living. If Christ is living in me, I have died to "my will, myself, and my dreams. My plans make no sense without Him." If Christ lives in me, "His will, His dreams, His plans are first. As the Robin Mark song goes, "All of my ambitions, hopes, and plans … I surrender these into your hands."

Aligning our personal resources, talents, and efforts with divine purposes enhances their effectiveness and value. What we possess becomes significantly more impactful when it is in line with God's plans and purposes. This alignment ensures that our assets and actions are not just fruitful on a personal level but also contribute meaningfully to a broader, spiritual mission. By harmonizing our endeavors with God's will, we maximize our potential to affect positive change and fulfill a higher purpose.

In the context of discipleship and the analogy of keeping one's spiritual house clean, this means dedicating all aspects of one's lifetime, talents, and treasures—in service and obedience to God's direction. It suggests that when one's endeavors are synchronized with God's desires, they are optimized for a meaningful and purposeful existence that not only benefits the individual but also enriches the community and fulfills divine objectives. This can be seen as an invitation to continuously seek and confirm one's alignment with divine will, ensuring that actions and possessions are used according to God's greater plan.

The Holy Spirit is not someone for us to use! Like an employee who works for me that I can call on when I need him. He wants to live in us and be the One who is in us. God is not a "Supersonic Server on Wheels" who rolls to your window, takes your order, then skates off to fill it. Nor is He a glorified Bell Hop we ask to carry our luggage, Who waits for a tip of thanksgiving.

Our God wants to live in intimate fellowship with us. He has created us to be Spirit-filled, gentle and compassionate people, whose purpose for living becomes communicating the good news of a kind and merciful God. We must make Spirit-fullness a preoccupation. Go after God with all your heart. Let go of things that hinder your holy pursuit if you ever hope to be the best version of your sanctified self. Billy Graham once said, "Wherever true Christianity has gone, Jesus's followers have performed acts of kindness, love, and gentleness." If you have received the Holy Spirit since you believed (Acts 19:2, KJV), what kind of fruit do they see growing on your tree? Sanctified believers know how to be kind to everyone, and to pray the right kind of prayers that reap the best possible answers.

> **Prayer Response:** *Loving Father, I invite you into my life today and surrender myself completely to You. Help me to become the-best-version-of-myself by seeking your will and becoming a living example of your love in the world.*[11] *Lord, I need Holy Spirit help to remain in a surrendered state as a living sacrifice, holy and pleasing to You (Rom.12:1). Help me to die daily to self and selfish desires, dreams, and devices. I am willing to forego the selfish, physical, and egotistical desires of this world and*

---
11 Play Like a Champion Today, "A Prayer for Transformation."

wholeheartedly seek the kingdom of God. My all on the altar of sacrifice I lay. In Jesus' name. Amen.

Model What You Mandate

Leaders must set the pace and model how to become disciple makers. Leaders should not just command others what to do what they are unwilling to do. We must model what we teach. By setting the pace and modeling disciple-making, leaders demonstrate their commitment to their teachings, inspiring others through their example. Rather than merely instructing, effective leaders embody the principles they wish to impart, fostering a culture of active participation and genuine growth among their followers.

This BHAG pushes us beyond tribal theology to core theology and comes directly from the lips of our Risen Savior. My mind did mental flashbacks to Cali, Colombia. The Spirit reaffirmed Pastor Herrera's impassioned plea, "We must change the function of the church—*to win souls for Christ*—and Adalberto's unforgettable words, *"I teach what I live!"* Do I? Do you? He allows no one to speak about church growth whose church is not growing. Now, there in Kigali, 7,478 nautical miles away, echoed the same discipleship theme—*model what you mandate*. It's an age old saying, "If you're going to talk the talk, you've got to walk the walk"—a modern version of old sayings like "actions speak louder than words" and "practice what you preach." Another early form of the expression was "walk your talk." In other words, "Act on your speech."[12]

Feeling convicted and desperately dependent, I journaled a cry for help. Now the Spirit was saying, I want you not only to "embrace the mission of your church—to make Christ-like disciples in the nations"—but also to exceed inactivity. Major Ian Thomas clarifies, "It is not inactivity, but Christ-activity; God in action accomplishing the divine end through human personality." Inactivity is like sitting in a rocking chair. It gives us something to do but gets us nowhere. "The

---

12 Website of Prof. Paul Brians, "Walk the Talk," Washington State University.

leaders' problems must be corrected first," Adalberto admonished. Whatever is keeping the leader from leading effectively, must be corrected. Attitude? Laziness? Inaction? Discouragement? Whatever keeps us from the central task of disciple-making must be corrected to get us moving in the right direction.

Beloved, God calls us to action, to rise from complacency, and to step boldly into the path He has prepared for us. When we seek His guidance, we must do so with the intent to act on it—promptly and fully—trusting Him with our steps, even when the way forward seems unclear.

Consider the promise of transformation that comes from such obedience. When we operate in total dependence on God, He becomes our strength, our wisdom, and our guide. He delights in turning things around when we move in faith, not hesitating, but trusting His leading completely.

Now is the time to move out of inactivity. Each of us has a sphere of influence—a unique opportunity to impact the culture and ethos around us for God's glory. By taking those initial steps today, we allow God to work through us, initiating change within us that ripples outward, affecting those we encounter.

Remember the way God transformed the early disciples—ordinary people who took extraordinary steps of faith. They didn't wait until they felt ready or had all the answers; they responded to Jesus' call and trusted that He would equip them along the way. Their actions, fueled by faith, catalyzed a movement that changed the world.

So, I urge you, dear friends, to take that leap of faith. Let God transform your heart and mind, and as you are changed, watch how He begins to change the world around you. Trust Him with your journey and see how quickly He can turn things around when you walk in His will.

Prayer Response: *Lord, forgive me if I have allowed prayer to compensate for my laziness and inaction. Cast out all despair, oh mighty God. Let your Spirit rush in. Give me clarity and courage. For I am yours. I confess that prayer and fasting, though they are essential, necessary, and commanded in the Scriptures, should in no way be a cover for laziness. Grant me a fresh resolve to be an active participant in Christ activity with You as you move. I refuse to talk the walk unless I actively walk it like I talk it. Through the power of Christ, Amen.*

The Bible Is Our Compass

I encourage you to ground your life in the steadfast principles and teachings found in Scripture. By immersing yourself in God's Word, you anchor your beliefs, values, and actions in a foundation that offers unwavering guidance and wisdom. In doing so, you draw upon a source of strength that can sustain you through life's tests and trials. Let the Bible be your compass, providing you with direction, purpose, and a clear path forward. Commit to living a life of integrity, compassion, and faithfulness, and watch as your actions resonate deeply with the spiritual truths you embrace. So ground your life in the truth that has stood the test of time, and let it elevate your journey.

Incorporating fasting into your spiritual practice can profoundly deepen your connection with God and enhance your receptiveness to His direction. Fasting, as a biblical discipline, assists in clearing the mind and spirit from distractions and earthly concerns, creating space for intensive prayer and meditation on God's Word.

As you dedicate yourself to aligning your preaching and teaching with God's intentions, consider regular fasting as a tool to heighten your spiritual awareness and strengthen your reliance on God. It can be a powerful act of humility and submission to His will, helping you to detach from worldly influences and focus more completely on seeking His guidance and wisdom.

Embrace fasting not just as a personal discipline, but also as a practice to potentially share and explore within your community of faith. It can encourage a collective spiritual renewal and unity, providing a solid foundation from which your congregation can grow together in faith and in their pursuit of God's plan. Through fasting, prayer, and faithful teaching, you can lead by example, showing how to live a life deeply rooted in spiritual disciplines and aligned with divine purposes.

Reflecting on whether "we really stand for holiness of heart and life and for aggressive evangelism" (H. Orton Wiley) requires a deep look at how our beliefs align with our actions. Are our lives and our community truly demonstrating the transformative power of holiness and actively engaging in sharing the gospel? This introspection involves examining not only individual behaviors but also communal efforts in evangelism, the consistency of our preaching versus our practices, and the overall impact of our ministry on others. If there are discrepancies between our declared values and our actual practices, it may be time to recommit and realign our actions to reflect our professed commitments more faithfully.

Do you truly believe it? It's essential to not only know your beliefs but also to understand deeply the reasons behind them. As a proud member of the Nazarene community, my conviction compels me to embrace my identity and the unique path I walk, while steadfastly upholding the profound teachings and principles of our faith.

In a world that often promotes bending rules for the sake of inclusion and tolerance, I stand firm. I choose not to manipulate biblical truths to fit contemporary narratives. Instead, I am committed to serving others with the unequivocal authority of Jesus Christ. My guidance comes not from personal desires or interpretations, but from a faithful adherence to the doctrine and practices upheld by my denomination.

This is not just about maintaining tradition—this is about an authentic expression of faith that does not waiver in the face of societal pressures. It's about engaging with the world courageously, grounded in the unshakeable foundation of our beliefs. Let us hold fast to what we profess, for this is how we demonstrate our true commitment to our faith and our God. "The Bible is tried and true…not just a starting point; it's the final authority when it comes to matters of faith and doctrine. It is the inspired Word of God. Truth with a capital T," as Mark Batterson tells. Never elevate tolerance above truth for we are called to "a higher standard than tolerance. It's called truth, and it's always coupled with grace."[13]

The inspired Word of God is the authority on which we base our beliefs and behavior. Make sure your beliefs and behaviors are rooted and grounded in Scripture. Be loyal to the tribe you have chosen. He might have gone on to caution against demonizing Bible-believing Christians in other tribes, but perhaps he understood that doctrinal diversity is almost limitless. When you join a particular denomination or church, make sure it clearly represents what you believe. If your core beliefs change as an elder or layperson, make a graceful not acrimonious nor litigious exit.

Elders take an oath at ordination—at least I did. Doctors take the Hippocratic Oath to refrain from causing harm or hurt; and to live an exemplary personal and professional life. Don't make it a hypocritical oath that ends up bringing harm and hurt. The Great Commission is not about proselytizing (changing the beliefs of the already saved); it is about making Christlike disciples of all nations (seeking the salvation of lost and broken people) of every ethnicity. Take your theological stance upon the Word of God that stands forever.

> **Prayer Response:** *Lord, convict me of any hypocrisy in my life and drive it away once and for all. Let there be no discrepancy between what I say I believe and how I behave. Lord, give me grace to understand that if I no longer believe what my church believes, I should seek a peaceful exit with a holy disposition that expresses the fruits of Your Spirit. Through the power of Christ, Amen.*

---

13 Mark Batterson, Whisper, 64.

A Place to Stand

We need a firm foundation for our beliefs. In a world where opinions and ideas are constantly evolving, holding on to settled and fixed points of belief can provide stability and consistency (Matt.24:35). From this vantage point we can discern which values and principles are essential and unchanging, serving as a compass amid shifting societal trends. This approach encourages critical thinking and reflection, allowing individuals to navigate new opinions with confidence and clarity, rather than being swayed by every emerging trend.

Archimedes, the famous Grecian mathematician, and inventor, said: "Give me a place to stand and a lever strong enough and I can move the world." Jesus asserted the trustworthiness of unchanging truth. Our understanding may change, but truth never changes. "The first thing to know about (His) word," the psalmist declared, "is that it is true" (Ps.119:160). It is a rock-solid place to stand because it *"stands firm in heaven forever"* (Ps.119:89, CEB).

The first quarter of the 21st century has seen the erosion of truth by "a lost and ever-more degraded generation." T.M. Moore explains, "We might be tempted to think that if only our churches were more like the world…our preaching less stringent and more soothing, our worship more 'enjoyable' and more like what lost folks are familiar with as forms of entertainment, our dress more casual, and our overall aspect and approach more relaxed and less imposing, then the world would be attracted to Jesus and believe. No," he responds emphatically. The "Spirit gives life; the flesh profits nothing. The words that I speak to you are spirit, and *they* are life" (Jn. 6.63).[14] *Sola Scriptura* is a solid rock on which to stand.

Few things are worth dying for, and most are not even worth suffering for. But God can bring us to a point of inner conviction which says regarding the truth, "For this I would be willing to die." For the Christian committed to God's Word, even from the earliest days of the

---

14 T.M. Moore, "Sola Scriptura," Scriptorium, The Fellowship of the Ailbe, May 13, 2023.

faith, compromise was never a viable alternative. "As you courageously stand on the truth of the Bible, anticipate that you will encounter opposition, but know that pleasing Almighty God is far more blessed than pleasing people."[15] The foundation upon which our faith is built is the Word of God. To attempt to build faith without the structural solidarity of sound doctrine leads to eventual frustration and disillusionment. So, screw your courage to the sticking place of God's unchanging Word and stand! "I stand alone on the Word of God, the B-I-B-L-E."

> **Prayer Response:** *Father, I ask you to give me courage to live and speak the truth unashamedly in love. Deliver me from fear of negative reaction by those consumed with worldly lies. May my life be characterized by a gentle kindness visible to all I encounter this day. Load the branches of my life with spiritual fruit. Use my life to perform loving acts of kindness and compassion I pray and give me the courage to be a good and faithful witness to Jesus, in word and in action, to bring Him praise, honor, and glory. In Jesus' name. Amen.*

"Give Me Your Hand"

It's important to recognize and address any feelings of superiority that may cause division. The richness of our faith traditions, including Wesleyan-Arminian perspectives, should contribute to the broader Christian dialogue rather than separate us. Recognizing our shared mission to fulfill the Great Commission, we must strive for unity and collaboration, focusing on the core theology that binds us together as believers. By emphasizing "Task" theology, as outlined in Matthew 28:19-20, we can unite in our call to be a missional people, working together to spread the love and teachings of Christ to all nations. Let's break down those walls of separation and embrace the strength found in a reformation of collaboration.

---

15 Wendy Boardman blog, "Pleasing God or Pleasing People?" July 2021.

UNLEASHING THE SUPERNATURAL

Practice "the protocol of the common camp" especially when you pray. Evangelical prayer ground is neutral ground made holy ground by the Spirit who is alive within us. If your heart is as my heart, give me your hand (2 Kings 10:15). Refuse to stand there with arms folded and fists clinched. Open your heart and hands in Christian love, compassion, and unity to all who serve Christ as Savior and Lord.

P. Douglas Small, President of *Project Pray*, opines, "One of the barriers to our fulfillment of the Great Commission is a lack of unity and collaboration between congregations." We will not lose an inch of ground by embracing fellow believers at the foot of the Cross. We just may have to remove our shoes because we are standing on holy ground. Holy ground is rendered sacred by the presence of God, who is the very essence of holiness. Holy ground has been described as "a place of invitation and revelation," a place of "strategic intersection," signals Karen Hardin. "It is the Father's offer to go into a new place" where "the natural intersects with the supernatural in a way that is completely unexpected." Such a "mission impossible" moment may occur the moment members of the Body of Christ begin to say, "Give me your hand." "This is your assignment, if you choose to accept it."[16]

Prayer Response: *Lord, You seem to be bringing the Body of Christ to a place of "strategic intersection." Enable us to leave our chariot and extend the right-hand of fellowship at the foot of the Cross. Bring us to the unity You prayed for in John 17, where You are supreme. Make us one, Lord. If I am guilty of breaking the Gospel protocol (Eph.4:5-6), I confess it now and ask You to enable me to find a way to cooperate with Christ followers in my city. Show me the Christian to whom You would have me extend a hand today. In Jesus' name. Amen.*

Achieving Next Level Prayer

In the oppressive heat of the packed room, the air thick with anticipation and resolve, the Regional Director stood forthrightly before

---

16 Karen Harden blog, "Seven Signs You Are On Holy Ground," March 30, 2018.

the gathered leaders—men and women marked by their resilience and dedication. His voice, fervent and compelling, pierced the heavy air, reverberating off the walls as he called on these leaders to elevate their spiritual disciplines to extraordinary levels. It was a summons to deep, persistently seeking God's face and will, crucial for the guidance and growth of their communities and churches.

Given the harsh realities of their environment—where many battle daily with the challenges of insufficient resources and food scarcity—the Director's message wisely emphasized the power of prayer over fasting. For these leaders, the primary tool available was the profound and persistent invocation for divine intervention and strength. The focus was clear: in a context where physical nourishment was often lacking, spiritual nourishment must become their fortitude, a source of both comfort and power.

Contrastingly, for others like myself, residing in the comfort of food security and abundance, the act of fasting introduces a unique spiritual depth. In societies marked by excess, fasting as a discipline sharpens one's spiritual senses, cutting through the noise and distractions of a materially saturated life. It becomes a deliberate act of deprivation, a physical metaphor for the spiritual stripping necessary to delve into deeper relational depths with God.

Fasting, in this view, is not just about abstaining from food but about a hunger for righteousness, an earnest pursuit of God's presence that transcends physical appetites. This disciplined vulnerability helps in cultivating a heightened awareness of our dependence on God, prompting a more fervent prayer life that reaches new levels of sincerity and intensity.

Driven by the Regional Director's impassioned plea, each context calls for its specific spiritual response: extraordinary prayer remains the common foundation, yet the practice of fasting differentiates in its application, tailored to the spiritual and physical realities of each community. This dual approach underscores a universal truth across diverse cultures—the profound need for an ever-deeper engagement with God, which both challenges and transcends our earthly conditions.

It is so important to be genuine before God, focusing not on the quantity or volume of prayer, but on its sincerity. In regions where scarcity sometimes forces fasting, prayer becomes an essential part of daily life. His message served as a reminder of the deep, authentic connection to be cultivated with God, transcending circumstances and anchoring faith in genuine devotion. And if we are to reap a global end-time harvest, it will be preceded by the sweet incense of passionate prayer.

My Cali experience reaffirmed in Kigali, birthed a vision for extraordinary prayer *and* fasting as an overstuffed American. Perhaps I didn't fully grasp the truth Cindy Barnes revealed when she said, "There are times when fervent prayer goes hand in hand with the added boost of fasting before God, (especially when you) have an unusual request that you are seeking an answer for." Extraordinary Prayer Requests (EPRs) are next level prayer requests. The Holy Spirit can go anywhere He wants to go. Any group, any church, any city.

Reflecting on the journey so far, I acknowledge with a sincere heart that I waited too long to call the churches I served to engage in extraordinary prayer, and even more so, in the vital practice of prayer and fasting. This realization weighs heavily on me, as I consider the profound impact these spiritual disciplines can have on a community's faith and action.

The power of collective prayer and fasting cannot be overstated—they are spiritual tools that can bring us closer to God, deepen our faith, and enhance our communal strength to face challenges. These practices are essential, not only as means of seeking divine guidance and intervention but also in fostering a spirit of unity and purpose within our congregations.

Looking forward, I am committed to not only integrating these disciplines into the life of the church but also to encouraging a vibrant culture of spiritual depth and reliance on God. It is never too late to renew our focus and dedication. Let us embrace prayer and fasting with renewed vigor, trusting that God will work mightily among us as we seek Him together with humble and contrite hearts. This is a clarion call to spiritual awakening, one that I hope will resonate deeply and stir us to action, for the benefit of our communities and the furtherance of the Gospel.

It's hard to admit that I paid lip service to prayer. I talked about prayer but truthfully, I did not pray much blaming busyness. I endeavored to produce first class "houses of preaching and singing" with excellence as our standard, but not true houses of prayer! Something had to change and as always it starts in the heart of the leader. Benjamin Pontius blogged, "Intercession is one of the greatest responsibilities (we) have – perhaps *the* greatest responsibility – to intercede for (our) people. Teach them, yes. Train them and counsel them, yes. Lead them in the study of Scripture and cast vision, yes. Guide them into the mission the Lord has called them to, yes. But above all pray for them. Pray over them. Pray with them. To fail in doing so is to sin."[17]

> **Prayer Response:** *Lord, I want to be in a praying church, but I haven't been the example in prayer I should be. I repent and ask for grace to incorporate prayer and fasting into my agenda. Start in me a renewed hunger and thirst for righteousness and begin to use me as a catalyst for prayer in my church. Clear away all the excuses of busyness I have used and enkindle a spirit of discipline in me that results in renewed fervency. With Samuel of old I pray, "Far be it from me that I should sin against the Lord by ceasing to pray"! In Jesus' name. Amen.*

---

[17] Benjamin Pontius, "The Poison of the Prayerless Leader," The Everlasting Fallout, December 7, 2013.

The Transforming Power of One Praying Person

At the April 2017 *Fusion Conference,* Brent Brooks of *One Cry* shared how God had sent him to a godless city, Reno, Nevada, nine years before to plant a church. Gambling and prostitution were openly advertised on the taxis and buses of Reno when he first arrived. Brent described it as "one of the most unlikely places in the USA for God to break out in revival." So, he joined citywide prayer efforts for the city crying out with other pastors, *"Why not here, Lord? You've done it in other places."* And God began to move and change everything. Today, houses of prostitution are not openly advertised. Now, church advertisements greet visitors. Prayer opens the door to transformation. "Pain can lead to prayer and prayer to providence and providence to praise," wrote Michael Milton. Prayer is known to "produce a resolution of purpose" for those who "embrace the Gospel that the things that have come against us are the very things that God uses to advance us."[18]

This is the transforming power of prayer. *"Just find one," God told Jeremiah, and heaven and earth will be moved (5:1).* Did Jeremiah look for just one other person who would agree in prayer with him? Or was no one upright? Could he not find one other person who cared? In Isaiah God looked for a single person who would stand in the gap to make a difference but found no one (Isaiah 59:15-16). So "God's arm brought victory upheld by (His own) righteousness."

Intercession demands a sacrifice of our time and life's focus. Do it and you will become an example of how to lay down your life for another. It's what friends of God do (John 15:13). Intercessory prayer allows us to carry the burden, or intervene, on another's behalf through prayer. There is not a more loving act of selflessness. God is still calling courageous believers to take Him at His Word and become intercessors who faithfully stand in the gap and seek His heart in prayer.

---

18 Michael Milton, "The Transforming Power of Prayer," Faith for Living, Inc., August 2, 2015.

Prayer Response: *Father, let me be the one who takes a hold of "the infinite grace at our disposal," on behalf of others, praying without ceasing. I know You will not fail to hear the prayer of those who intentionally stand in the gap as intercessors for their homes, their families, their churches, their cities, and for this nation. Through the powerful name of Jesus. Amen.*

9

Miraculous Breakthroughs

Throughout history, the acts of prayer and fasting have been cornerstones of spiritual life, providing avenues for personal transformation and divine intervention. These spiritual disciplines represent more than mere rituals; they are profound expressions of faith, through which believers lay down their natural desires to seek deeper communion with God. In this pursuit, we find that prayer and fasting are not just acts of piety but are powerful catalysts for miraculous breakthroughs.

Expecting miraculous breakthroughs because of such spiritual dedication does not stem from wishful thinking or religious formulae; rather, it is a recognition of the dynamic interaction between human devotion and divine power. As we surrender our physical needs and intensify our spiritual focus, we create space for God to move mightily in and through our lives. This intentional deprivation and pointed supplication clear the way for clarity, divine encounters, and the supernatural altering of our circumstances.

As we conclude this exploration into the potent combination of prayer and fasting, we prepare to witness compelling stories that attest to the miraculous power unleashed through these spiritual disciplines. These narratives not only serve to inspire and uplift but also offer tangible evidence of how deeply these practices can impact the human experience. Through real-life testimonies, we will see how barriers are broken, heavens are opened, and divine interventions transform lives in profound and undeniable ways. Let these stories fill you with faith and expectation, inviting you to embrace the supernatural possibilities that await those who earnestly seek the divine through prayer and fasting.

Prayer Response: *Almighty Father, You are the God of the breakthrough! I come before you today petitioning for a spiritual breakthrough in my life. I confess that I have been struggling against recurring sins, doubts, fears, and feelings of defeat. I feel stuck in stagnant patterns that I cannot seem to overcome on my own. I need your mighty power to break every chain and set me free.*[1]

One Man's Obedience

True love for God is demonstrated by keeping His commands, which are not burdensome for those born of God, as they have the strength to overcome the world through their faith, according to 1 John 5:3-4. This aligns with John C. Maxwell's principle that having the right vision at the right time leads to success. By faithfully adhering to God's commands and maintaining a clear vision rooted in faith, individuals are empowered to achieve spiritual victory and success in their lives.

Our speaker on Thursday night at the 2006 East Africa Field Holiness Convention was a tall Kenyan whom I will refer to as Ezekiel. He had recently arrived from the frontlines of spreading the Kingdom in the Horn of Africa. His soul-stirring message centered around a

---

[1] Daniel Naranjan, "Prayer For Breakthrough," Divinedisclosures.com, August 19, 2024.

question he found himself contemplating as he approached his fiftieth birthday. A year and a half earlier, he and his family had been enjoying what he called a "comfortable life in Kenya." As Ezekiel explained, "If you own a cow in Kenya, you will never go hungry." However, he soon began to feel God's call to carry the Gospel to Southern Sudan. After discussing it with his family, they made the decision to sell their cow and set out for the Sudan, trusting in God's provision.

"Where should I start?" Ezekiel asked the Lord.

"Drive east until you no longer see any cars," came the reply.

He obeyed and joined God in gathering souls in a war-torn region. Astonishingly, his efforts led to what became known as "The Miracle Movement." In just eighteen months, 243 churches were established, and that number grew to over 1,200 in the following years. When a man of God achieves so much in such a short time and continues to ask, *"What else can I do?"* it shows he is truly passionate about God's work. If we allow the Holy Spirit to instill this question deeply in our minds and hearts, we can accomplish more than we ever imagined.

If you are willing to be weak with the weak, vulnerable with the vulnerable, and powerless with the powerless, your "what else" is the next right thing God inspires you to do. For every follower of Jesus, the next right thing is clear: "Do whatever he tells you" (John 2:5 NIV).[2] In this region, where the supernatural seems interwoven with everyday experiences, the faithful are reminded of the power of leaning not on their understanding but wholly on the providential lead of Jesus Christ. Prayer and fasting thus serve as both the medium and the message, compelling believers to strip away reliance on worldly strength and instead venture into a life astonishingly led by the Holy Spirit.

Prayer Response: *Lord I ask You today for a fresh infusion of logic-defying faith. I am a little low on the faith meter. I long to experience Your supernatural miracles, but*

---

2 The reader is directed to my book Dancing with the Impossible, West Bow Press, 2023, for a book chock full of next right things that resulted in obedient servants achieving extraordinary success.

it requires that I have faith. Grow my mustard-seed-like faith into mountain-moving faith. Strengthen my faith and help me grow closer to You so I may experience Your wonders in my life. Open my eyes to a fresh realization that I can do anything You ask of me through Spirit power unleashed in me. In Jesus' name. I pray, Amen.

The Birthing of a Movement

As the number of churches grew exponentially, so did the evidence of God's hand at work. Each story of change, each new gathering of believers, became a testament to what can occur when a community turns its heart toward God, relying on Him completely. These narratives from the Horn of Africa inspire all to seek out divine encounters through a disciplined pursuit of extraordinary prayer and fasting, encouraging a global audience to marvel at the depth of God's creative orchestration in leading His people toward greater faith and unity.

The question, "What kinds of churches are we planting?" frequently arises, prompting a thorough examination of the qualities, characteristics, and spiritual orientations that define these new faith communities. In the Horn of Africa, a region woven with vibrant cultures and deep spirituality, there lie stories that illuminate the profound effects of spiritual practices like prayer and fasting. Here, amidst this dynamic backdrop, one can discover churches arising rapidly, an unfolding that seems almost miraculous in its breadth and speed.

These communities, sprouting extensively across Ethiopia and beyond within just a year, reflected a significant movement, a wave of spiritual awakening that did not stem merely from human efforts. Residents and visitors alike find themselves mere observers, witnessing the evidence of something that transcends ordinary explanation—movements of faith that redefine communities and transform lives.

The emergence of these churches symbolizes not only growth in numbers but a deeper, communal journey into faith practices that challenge the physical and encourage the spiritual. In these places, prayer and fasting are not outdated rites but vital acts that open doors to divine intervention and personal transformation.

The accounts from this region resonate with a message of hope and a testament to the unstoppable force of collective belief. As one delves into these narratives, it becomes clear that these are not mere coincidences or natural progressions but are, potentially, the results of divine forces at play, affirming the transformative power of devout spiritual engagement.

These tales from the Horn of Africa are a vivid illustration of how deeply faith can influence reality, inviting us to explore the limitless potential of the supernatural in our own lives. While enroute to a conference, a pastor observed a significant number of unreached individuals during a transportation delay and, after prayerful consideration, decided to establish a church to meet their spiritual needs, demonstrating a strategic needs-based approach to church planting. Across the river, an evangelist shared the gospel with the local community, leading to the formation of another church, emphasizing the impact of personal evangelism and direct gospel outreach in fostering new congregations. Both examples highlight proactive responses to spiritual voids in different areas, underscoring the commitment to expanding faith communities by recognizing and addressing unmet spiritual needs.

God often chooses individuals who may not outwardly display exceptional skills or leadership abilities, utilizing those who are available and willing to serve. The crucial element here is obedience. Extraordinary things occur when we pray and fast for bold, holy, audacious goals, and when we adhere to the three GC's: the Great Commandment (Love), the Great Commission (Make disciples), and the Great Commitment (Prayer). "We must allow Jesus to work through us to bear witness to the world," wrote Alex Nolette in his blog. "Being a witness is not simply an item on a to-do list; it is the very identity created by the Holy Spirit in those who have placed their trust and faith in Jesus."[3]

---

3 Alex Nolette, "Living as a Witness: The Holy Spirit & Evangelism," Mercy Hill Church, September 7, 2016.

We should be an active part of God's movement, allowing it to unfold naturally. God will accomplish His plans with or without our involvement. In the light of the harvest movement in the Horn of Africa, a new understanding of what defines a church has arisen: "any gathered group of believers with a designated pastoral leader." A church is not merely a building; it is a community of people, with Christ as the head of any assembly of believers. A significant movement in response to the Spirit's outpouring should naturally lead to evangelism. The energies of Christianity must be directed outward towards a lost and broken world. One of the primary reasons the Spirit was given at Pentecost was to empower the Church to be personal witnesses for Christ. Indeed, this is the most compelling evidence of the Holy Spirit's power.

Prayer Response: *"Righteous Savior, as I look out over (my) city, I see so many who are lost and afraid. And yet in my own strength, it feels like there is nothing I can do. I am shy. I am timid. Father, increase my faith. Give me the boldness I need to fill this city with the glorious hope of eternal life in Your Son, Jesus. Amen."*[4]

Purposeful Obedience

Ecclesiastes 11:1 encourages the act of casting your bread upon the waters, suggesting that taking risks or making generous or faithful investments will yield returns in due time. This idea is complemented by the notion that servants of the Lord should be ready and willing to act with cheerfulness, even when their actions might seem foolish or be mocked by others. True faith often involves moving forward with trust and optimism, despite external skepticism, believing that such actions will eventually bear fruit. Both concepts emphasize the virtue of stepping out in faith and generosity, trusting that positive outcomes will follow.

The stories emerging from this miracle-filled region following Ezekiel's acts of obedience, are nothing short of astounding. Purposeful

---

[4] Personalized from ConnectUS, "23 Powerful Prayers for Evangelism," May 14, 2020.

obedience creates an incredible ripple effect, akin to our Ecclesiastes 11:1 moment. As we *"cast our bread upon the waters,"* it returns to us with countless blessings in abundance. The Contemporary English Version of this verse states, *"Be generous, and someday you will be rewarded."* Ezekiel's generous actions led to abundant blessings, demonstrating the profound fulfillment found in purposeful obedience.

The 243 churches that Ezekiel planted grew nearly fourfold. Attendance soared from zero to 60,000 in just three years, with most of the attendees being new converts surrounded by those hostile to Christ and Christianity. As Tertullian once said, "The blood of the martyrs is the seed of the church." A Rwandan pastor was tragically burned alive in his car by persecutors, yet whenever a house church leader fell, someone else rose to the occasion. In one heart-wrenching incident, fourteen people gathered for worship in a Somalian house church were slaughtered. Aweise expressed, *"It's hard, but we trust the Sender."* In one village, fires destroyed everything except for the properties of the Nazarenes. "It burned around the Nazarene's grass," leading to the miraculous establishment of 35 new churches shortly thereafter.

In 2006-07, the Africa Region experienced an extraordinary rate of church growth, averaging four new church plants each day. Within three years, over 100,000 new believers joined the faith. This remarkable event might be one of the most significant movements in Christian history, as described by a firsthand visitor: "This may be unprecedented." Martin Luther once said, "We're not saved by faith and works. But we are saved by a faith that works." How should you respond to this call for action? Pastor Adrian Rogers outlined "Five How's" for a faith that works: with intelligent, intentional, immediate, inflexible, and impassioned obedience. He concluded by saying, "Because God is sovereign, there can be no refusal and no rebuttal. The only alternative to obedience is disobedience."[5]

Prayer Response: *Lord, I haven't always readily obeyed. I've questioned, doubted, even over thought what*

---
5 Adrian Rogers, "The Experience of Obedience," OnePlace.com.

You've asked of me. Forgive me. Holy Spirit, give me a heart to obey. I want to work out my salvation and Your teachings in every aspect of my life. I will purposely obey knowing that I will have to give an account for my life and that You're watching the decisions that I'm making. Grant me strength to continue to trust You and walk in your ways. Let your will be second nature so that all my actions are pleasing to You. In Jesus' name. Amen.

"Eye-Popping Miracles"

The wisest man who ever lived encouraged the act of casting our bread upon the waters (Eccl. 11:1), suggesting that taking risks or making generous or faithful investments will yield returns in due time. This idea is complemented by the notion that servants of the Lord should be ready and willing to act with cheerfulness, even when their actions might seem foolish or be mocked by others. True faith often involves moving forward with trust and optimism, despite external skepticism, believing that such actions will eventually bear fruit. Both concepts emphasize the virtue of stepping out in faith and generosity, trusting that positive outcomes will follow.

Extraordinary prayer and fasting should inspire us to be devoted to God and eager to follow His commands. When stubbornness is cast aside, and we are driven to be fully faithful, we enter a realm where astonishing transformations can occur. A compelling story from Ethiopia serves as a living testament to the unleashed power of God. The names in the story are fictional, but the events are true. Tariku was the only member of his family to receive an education. During his time in school, his father was killed. According to cultural expectations, not avenging his father's death would bring great shame upon him. After completing his education, Tariku became a teacher, was elected to the town council, and was entrusted with a machine gun.

Tariku stormed out, fueled by a wildfire of vengeance, clutching a pistol with deadly intentions. He was out for blood, the blood of four men who had torn his world apart by murdering his father. But as he zeroed in on his first target, a sobering thought cooled his fury: eight bullets might fall short in a clash against the killers and any witnesses who could cross his path. Frustration mounting, he headed back home, determined to upgrade his arsenal to a machine gun—death's symphony at his fingertips.

Yet, unbeknownst to him, God had a plot twist in store. His nephew, Sesay, wide-eyed and quivering, intercepted him, petrified by the darkness consuming his uncle. With a voice trembling yet earnest, Sesay urged Tariku to ease his seething wrath with a simple act—a meal. With reluctant steps, Tariku sat, anger sizzling within, only to be met with an abrupt, life-altering accident—a burst of gunfire from his pocket that shattered his femur and his mission.

Confined to a sterile hospital bed, Tariku faced grim news: his leg would need amputation. Crushed by despair, he sought escape in the numbness of sleep, swallowing eight pills with a grim resolve to surrender his life rather than face the future crippled and defeated. But in defiance of his own expectations, he awakened 40 hours later, an IV snaking into his arm, with a singular, burning question: *"Why am I alive?"*

This was not merely fortune smiling down on him but the prevenient grace of God. Tariku's survival was no accident—it was a divine signal, an invitation to a journey of discovery, to break free from the suffocating chains of honor-bound revenge. He was meant for more than the relentless cycle of retribution, designed for a purpose greater than he had ever imagined. In time, he would unearth this purpose, dedicating his life to a profound calling.

Have you uncovered God's purpose for your life? We are not here to merely drift through existence, slaves to our own desires and cultural dictates. We are here to connect deeply with our Creator, to experience the exquisite joy of knowing Him and living out our divine purpose every single day. Consider this moment the beginning of your own journey to discover what you are truly meant to do.

> **Prayer Response:** *My Savior and Lord, "I come before you on this beautiful day, to worship You, Almighty God. You are high and lifted up. Please, pour out Your power and love upon me. Oh Lord, I ask for supernatural transformation in my sinful life today. Change my heart. Guide my life. Make me new, and born again, through Christ. Mold me into who I am truly meant to be."[6] In Jesus' name. Amen.*

The Kiss of Grace

"I will give you a new heart and put a new spirit in you; I will remove from you your heart of stone and give you a heart of flesh" (Ezekiel 36:26, NIV). These words echo with the promise of renewal, assuring us that no matter how firmly the chains of our past may grip us, we are not destined to remain in their hold. Transformation is possible, inviting us to embrace each new heartbeat and breath of hope, stepping toward a future unburdened by what once was.

Confined to his bed, a friend gave Tariku a New Testament. As he started reading it, he heard Jesus speaking to him in Amharic that night, assuring him that he was healed. Embracing this miracle, he left the hospital on crutches a few days later. One day, a crutch slipped from his hand, and he took three steps before realizing he no longer needed it. When someone later asked if he had ever given his life to Christ, Tariku admitted he hadn't and decided to do so at that moment. However, shortly afterward, he was plagued by visions of his father's murderers mocking him, suggesting that as a Christian, he was too weak to avenge his father's death. Overwhelmed by shame and torment, Tariku felt that he couldn't remain a Christian and resolved to confront the first of the murderers. He had not yet developed the faith

---

[6] Cheryce Rampersad, "Prayer: The Supernatural Power Of A Transformed Mind!," ChristiansTT, February 20, 2023.

to believe he could rise above the wrongs done to him by others.

In a sniper's position, he had a clear shot and attempted to take it, but the gun jammed. After unjamming it, he still had a clear shot and tried again, yet the gun jammed once more. Frustrated, he retreated into the bushes, took the gun apart, reassembled it, and tested it; this time, it worked perfectly. Returning to his position, he took aim with a clear shot, fired, and experienced another jam. In that decisive moment, he abandoned the gun and wholeheartedly gave his life to Christ. Sometimes, it takes a miraculous intervention, but transformation is always possible. I firmly believe that people can change when they have a life-altering encounter with Jesus Christ. Men and women who repent of their sins can become new creations (2 Cor. 5:17). Tariku discovered, as every born-again believer does, that "When you meet Jesus, everything changes. When the truth of the Gospel truly encounters your heart and life, you cannot remain the same" (Daniel Im).[7]

I love this analogy: "A Christian isn't like a tadpole transforming into a frog. While the creature undergoes a series of changes, it remains fundamentally the same. Instead, a Christian resembles more closely a frog that receives the kiss of grace and transforms into a prince. We are changed radically and dramatically!" If anyone ever received this profound kiss of grace, it was Tariku. It's "the perfect kiss," and those who experience it discover the dimension of Christian living that Jesus refers to as "easy and light." As James Richards highlights, "We still kiss," implying that "Jesus has completed the work, so relax and let His grace transform your heart."[8]

Prayer Response: *Lord, transform me—not for my benefit alone, but for the benefit of my family, my church, and all who know me. Do your work in me—molding me, making me, shaping me, changing me, to be the new creation you have called me to be in Jesus Christ. Amen.*

---

[7] Posted on Pinterest by Paul Dazet.
[8] James B. Richards, We Still Kiss, Synopsis on Amazon, 2002.

Write Your Own Story

As we pen the chapters of our own life stories, taking a leaf out of Abraham's book, as recounted in Hebrews 11:8, can guide us profoundly. Abraham's experience is a testament to unwavering faith and obedience. He ventured forth without ever laying eyes on the promised land, relying wholly on God's assurances and direction. His journey teaches us the true essence of obedience: it's about more than just passive compliance; it's about actively living in tune with the guidance we receive from the Holy Spirit (John 16:13). When we choose to listen and act on the Spirit's prompts, we are aligning our narrative with God's divine will, just as Abraham did. It's a call to walk paths paved with trust and faith, propelled by a vision seen not through our eyes but through our spirit.

The Rwandan woman who sang a special song on the night Ezekiel preached shared her testimony of how the Lord guided her back to Rwanda after the 1994 massacre. She recounted with tears in her eyes how "the smell of death" was almost unbearable and how human remains were everywhere. In desperation, she asked the Lord, "What should I do?" and heard Him say, *"Sow seeds of love and peace."* After her song, a man who responded to the invitation shared his own testimony of fleeing Ethiopia to escape death. He had settled in Kenya and was living a comfortable life. With tears and deep emotion, he managed to say, *"Jesus, if you want me to go back to Ethiopia, I'll go."* My friend, Larry McKain, then President of New Church Specialties, and I joined the Africans in humble prayer on our knees, saying, *"Send us wherever you will."*

Do you long to see God work wonders so transformative that they continue to inspire awe and faith in future generations? Imagine witnessing divine acts that emerge in response to a community united in repentance, humility, and fervent prayer. This vision of holiness is not only the beacon of hope for Africa but also the foundational promise for America.

There came a pivotal day, as I surveyed the horizon of what might be the final quarter of my life, when I felt a profound calling. It was a summons to dedicate my remaining days to deeper service: to live as a beacon of true servanthood, to lead by example, to mentor the next generation, and to ardently preach the undeniable truth of scriptural holiness.

Now, as I navigate the crucial final stretch—my own "gun lap"—the call has deepened. I am driven to become a "mentor in print," committing my accumulated wisdom to writing. Through these words, I aim not just to educate but to ignite a spiritual fire in others, encouraging a life rich in holiness and devotion.

Join me in this sacred journey, where together we endeavor to forge a legacy not just steeped in history, but one that energizes the future with the awe-inspiring power and presence of God. Remember, blessings and benefits are invariably linked to obedience—a truth profoundly encapsulated in "Life Lesson 21: Obedience always brings blessings."[9] Let's commit to this path of obedience so that we may unlock the full spectrum of God's blessings.

Pastor Micah Sturm reminds us that the disciplined life we are called to is not merely an obligation, but a daily pilgrimage marked by loving obedience, a deep devotion to the Lord, and an unwavering service to humanity. Embracing loving obedience propels us into new realms of effectiveness and productivity, transforming us into vital instruments of divine will.

Echoing this timeless insight, the words of John Calvin from the 16th century resonate with clarity and truth: "We cannot rely on God's promises without obeying His commands." This profound connection between divine promise and our active obedience underscores that while we may not be capable of doing everything, we are always capable of doing something. That 'something' is neither optional nor trivial; it is essential. We are called to act, to make a difference, and

---

9 Charles Stanley, "Life Principle 21: Obedience Always Brings Blessings," TV Sermon, November 1, 2019.

through our every effort, no matter how small, to echo God's infinite love and justice in the world.

Embarking on a journey of spiritual growth doesn't require you to be a perfect saint, if such a thing ever exists. Instead, engage earnestly in the practices of prayer and fasting, focusing your heart on purposeful obedience. You might be surprised at how significantly God can work through you when you commit to these disciplines with sincerity and faith.

> **Prayer Response:** *Speak, Lord. I'm open to hear from You today; yes, Lord, even the most unusual and seemingly illogical instructions. Direct my life and service to You today. You've promised to be with me all the way as I seek to carry out Your will and plan for my life. Though it be hard, Jesus, I will do what You tell me to do; even when it doesn't make sense because I trust You and am learning to lean hard on You. In Jesus' name. Amen.*

Embracing the Impossible

As I bring this little book to a close just six days before Christmas, I am challenged by Matthew's clarifying word: *"All of this happened to fulfill what the Lord had said through His prophet: 'The virgin will conceive and give birth to a son, and they will call him Immanuel,' which means 'God with us.'"* (Matthew 1:22-23 NLT). You did not pick up this book by chance. I like to think of it more as a rendezvous with old spiritual disciplines that if adopted with fresh new enthusiasm and commitment, you will look back and say, *"That's why, or better, that's how I successfully navigated the twists and turns in my life."* Despite the challenges and complications, you have lived to see the fulfillment of God's promise—a promise that reassures us that through prayer and fasting, nothing is impossible.

Deborah Rosenkranz articulately outlined the complications behind the Christmas story:

1. Mary found herself pregnant by an "unknown."
2. Joseph faced deep hurt and the whispers of gossip swirling around them.
3. The financial instability of the nation weighed heavily on them.
4. They were forced to leave their home just when they longed for comfort and safety.
5. When they sought refuge, there was no room for them; they felt unwelcome and alone.[10]

I trust that a new understanding of the supernatural is emerging in your journey of faith. From God's perspective, nothing in your life is impossible! If you embrace the impossible, He can enable you to move from overwhelmed to empowered. God specializes in turning the impossible into possible. Don't look back. Look forward to the new things He will do in you and through you (Isa. 43:18-19) embracing the possible with Christ (Phil.4:13).

As you reflect on your life, you may feel overwhelmed, thinking, "Everything has gone wrong; how can this possibly end well?" Keep straining forward, one step at a time. It's important to remember that, in due time, you will see the truth. Jesus was born to show us that through Him, the impossible becomes possible!"

One more thing. Immanuel means "God with us." So, whatever challenge lies before you, maintain your trust in divine possibility. And because He's with you, He invites you to write your own miraculous story. God is with you! In your greatest mess and your biggest chaos, you can trust that what seems like a deviation from the plan may just be the beginning of your greatest miracle.

Christmas embodies this message: "What starts out complicated often ends with divine miracles!" It's a time to believe in the One who makes the impossible possible—especially for you! So, as you pray and fast, remember that when things seem most impossible, you are inching forward trusting divine possibility.

---

10 Deborah Rosenkranz, "This Happened So That…" A Miracle Every Day, December 19, 2024.

Prayer Response: *Heavenly Father, as I come before You today, I seek Your presence with a humble heart. I acknowledge that You are the God of the impossible, the One who transforms our lives through Your supernatural power. I understand that through prayer and fasting, I can draw closer to You and open my life to the miraculous.*

Lord, I ask that You ignite a fervent spirit within me as I engage in prayer and fasting. Help me to focus my heart and mind on You, seeking Your guidance and wisdom in every aspect of my life. May this time of devotion cleanse my soul and strengthen my faith, allowing me to fully trust in Your plans.

I pray for breakthrough in the areas where I feel stuck, for healing where there is pain, and for provision where there is lack. Let Your supernatural intervention flow into my life and help me to witness Your glory in ways I have never imagined.

Holy Spirit, guide me as I seek You earnestly. Transform my expectations, enlarging my vision to see the possibilities that lie ahead. Grant me patience and perseverance, knowing that through this spiritual journey, I am aligning my will with Yours.

Father, unleash Your miracles in my life. May Your strength be made perfect in my weakness, and may I experience the fullness of Your love and grace. I trust that You are working behind the scenes, orchestrating every detail for my good.

Thank You for hearing my prayer and for being with me in this sacred time of fasting and prayer. I believe that with You, all things are possible, and I eagerly anticipate the marvelous works You will perform in my life. In Jesus' name, I pray, Amen.

AFTERWORD

Almighty God has designed us to be supernatural beings, drawing our strength, power, and might not from ourselves but from Him. The wealthy often depend on their talents, resources, and financial plans like insurance and retirement accounts to address immediate issues and secure their future. But as believers, where does our reliance lie? We turn to Almighty God's power and supernatural strength, which is fundamentally why we engage in prayer and fasting.

Someone asked rhetorically, "What is the first tool in your tool kit?" Asking ourselves about the first tool we reach for in times of need can be revealing. Do we grab our phones, or do we turn to God's throne in prayer? Our success or failure often hinges on whether we tap into the supernatural power available to us through prayer. Ephesians 6:18 urges us to *"pray at all times,"* yet the comforts of prosperity can sometimes weaken our dedication to prayer. As we grow accustomed to self-reliance and self-sufficiency, we risk letting these qualities replace our spiritual source of strength.

I frequently recount an enlightening story shared by P. Douglas Small, who experienced a striking interaction with a successful church planter during a School of Prayer event. When Dr. Small challenged the pastor to integrate more prayer into his leadership, the pastor's response was both shocking and revealing. He said, "I built this church from nothing to 300 members without prayer. Perhaps if I aim to grow it to 600, then I'll consider praying." This statement vividly underscores the often-undervalued role of prayer and fasting in achieving and sustaining success, highlighting a prevalent mindset that may overlook spiritual foundations in favor of apparent self-sufficiency.

Self-sufficiency can often lead us into a profound trap, one vividly illustrated in Habakkuk 3:17, where despite the prophet's relentless efforts and dedication, he faces a barren reality with no fruit, oil, or livestock—symbols of his labor turning into despair. This poignant scenario prompts us to examine our own lives.

Have you found yourself tirelessly striving, yet feeling as though you're grasping at air, with your efforts yielding no tangible results? If you rely solely on your capabilities, detached from divine guidance, it can lead you down an exhausting and unfruitful pathway. Habakkuk's "even though" experience serves as a powerful alarm: self-sufficiency without a deeper, spiritual anchor often leads to disillusionment. *"... Yet I will rejoice in the Sovereign Lord my strength"* (3:18-19), declared Habakkuk. This outlook can help steer us away from barrenness and toward dependence on God alone. Place you trust in the Lord, and you will access supernatural strength that deepens your connection with God and enriches your spiritual journey.

Perhaps, like Habakkuk, you feel that *"nothing has been seen yet,"* but keep believing and you'll be as *"surefooted as a deer, able to tread upon the heights"* (Hab. 3:19). If you've been relying solely on your own strength, consider following Habakkuk's lead by trusting and rejoicing in the Lord during the wait, making a conscious choice to please God—a choice that underscores your faith. You may not see results immediately, but that doesn't mean they won't manifest. Maybe God is waiting for you to relinquish your self-reliance and admit, *"It's not by might or power"* (Zech. 4:6). Embracing this mindset sooner can bring peace while you wait.

This is precisely why extraordinary prayer and fasting are so crucial; they acknowledge our weaknesses and our need for God. Letting go of self-sufficiency to embrace our spiritual need is essential because human effort alone often leads to little fruit (3:17). Remember, God's supernatural power can transform situations, urging us to forsake all confidence in human wisdom and strength, and seek fulfillment in Christ alone. We must disconnect from the illusory self-sufficiency to tap into God's transformative power, which reminds us, *"It's not by might nor by power, but by My Spirit!"* (Zechariah 4:6).

UNLEASHING THE SUPERNATURAL

Lives devoid of the supernatural are essentially superficial. If we can explain our existence without attributing all the credit to God, we have yet to fully tap into the extensive supernatural possibilities He has for us. Staying fixated on human capabilities—our gifts, abilities, organizational skills, planning, or strategies—will yield only modest results at best. Paul articulated this powerfully: *"I can do all things!"* but he quickly clarified, *"through Christ who strengthens me"* (Phil. 4:13). Put no confidence in the flesh, but we have divine power at work in us for life and godliness and supernatural Kingdom success! (2 Pet.1:3). If we believe we can navigate life on our own, relying solely on ourselves rather than on Him, He allows us the freedom to fail. Our true strength and success come from aligning with God's Spirit.

The redemptive work to which God calls us transcends human knowhow. Samuel Chadwick, one of the greatest preachers of English Methodism, profoundly noted, "The world will never believe in a religion in which there is no supernatural power. A rationalized faith, a socialized Church, and a moralized gospel may gain applause, but they awaken no conviction and win no converts." To truly engage with and advance the mission that God has laid out for us, it's imperative that we recognize the limitations of our own human efforts and the necessity of divine intervention. Our strength alone is insufficient for the tasks God calls us to; instead, we must lean into the support and empowerment provided by the Holy Spirit. It is the Holy Spirit that endows us with capacities far beyond our natural limits, enabling us to break through barriers of darkness that seem impenetrable by human means alone.

This supernatural power of the Holy Spirit is not merely an aid or a booster; it is the very essence of our ability to effect real change and bring light where there is darkness. The influence of the Holy Spirit in our endeavors isn't just helpful—it's crucial. It is through this divine power that we witness true miracles and transformations in our world, as the Holy Spirit acts not only within but also all around us, reshaping circumstances and touching hearts in ways that are beyond human capability.

However, the full exploration of the depths and implications of the Holy Spirit's power and its integration into our daily lives and missions is a vast subject that likely surpasses what can be encapsulated in a single discussion or treated adequately in brief. Delving into how the Holy Spirit operates, how we can more effectively collaborate with this divine force, and understanding the breadth of its impact, indeed warrants a more extensive examination—perhaps extensive enough to fill another entire book.

This exploration would involve a systematic study of scriptural insights, theological frameworks, and personal testimonies to form a comprehensive understanding of how the Holy Spirit moves and works. It would also look at practical ways believers can cultivate a deeper sensitivity and responsiveness to the Spirit's leadings, ensuring that our missions are not just carried out under our own steam but are truly Spirit-led and Spirit-empowered operations. Such an investigation is essential for anyone seeking to operate not out of mere human ambition or effort but in alignment with God's greater plan and power.

www.ingramcontent.com/pod-product-compliance
Lightning Source LLC
Chambersburg PA
CBHW062208080426
42734CB00010B/1843